THE ILLUSTRATED HANCOCK

THE ILLUSTRATED
HANCOCK

with a commentary by ROGER WILMUT

Macdonald
Queen Anne Press

A Queen Anne Press BOOK

© Roger Wilmut, 1986, 1987

First published in Great Britain in 1986 by
Queen Anne Press, a division of
Macdonald & Co (Publishers) Ltd
Greater London House, Hampstead Road
London NW1 7QX
This edition published in 1987 by
Queen Anne Press

A BPCC plc Company

Cover photographs: BBC (*front*)
                                Don Smith/Radio Times (*back*)

British Library Cataloguing in Publication Data

The Illustrated Hancock.
    1. Hancock, Tony   2. Comedians — Great
Britain — Biography
I. Wilmut, Roger
791'.092'4   PN2598.H23

ISBN 0-356-14781-9

Typeset by Leaper & Gard Ltd, Bristol, England
Printed and bound in Great Britain by
R.J. Acford, Chichester, Sussex

CONTENTS

ACKNOWLEDGEMENTS

First, thanks are due to the interviewees quoted in the text: Alan Simpson, Ray Galton, Eric Sykes, Dennis Main Wilson, Duncan Wood, Hugh Lloyd and Alan Tarrant. The following quotes from some of the above are taken from unused sections of the interviews conducted by Derek Bailey for the BBC Television *Omnibus* programme on Hancock broadcast on 26 April 1985, and are used by kind permission of the BBC and the interviewees: Galton and Simpson (pages 26, 55 and 124); Main Wilson (pages 23 and 25); Lloyd and Wood. My thanks to Derek Bailey (the director of the *Omnibus* documentary) and to Heather McCubbin for access to the original soundtracks of the interviews. The remaining quotes are taken from interviews done by the author.

Special thanks are due to Ray Galton and Alan Simpson for their permission to use quotations from their scripts; also to Roger Hancock for permission to quote from the ATV series and to Thorn EMI Screen Entertainment Limited for permission to quote from *The Rebel* and from *The Punch and Judy Man*.

Thanks are also due to Tessa le Bars; to Roger Hancock for access to photos; to Peter Copeland and D. Jeremy Stevenson for the loan of sound recordings; and to picture researcher Kathy Lockley.

Roger Wilmut
May 1986

INTRODUCTION

Television has always been essentially an ephemeral medium; programmes, once transmitted and perhaps once repeated, tended to disappear from public view for ever. However, the emergence of the domestic video recorder and the pre-recorded 'videogram' changed all that, and it was natural that the BBC in particular should take advantage of this new medium to make some of the best of its output available once again. It might have seemed surprising that among the glossy colour productions were a number of half-hour comedies which were over twenty-five years old and which featured a performer who had been dead for seventeen years, and that these programmes were subsequently repeated on television in peak time; but the name of the performer alone was sufficient explanation — Tony Hancock.

Despite the fact that these programmes had not been seen for many years, Hancock's popularity remained undimmed since his peak in the late 1950s. Long-playing records from his radio shows were still selling steadily; three books had been written on his life and work; there had recently been a major television documentary on him; and also two solo plays purporting to examine his inner conflicts. No other comedian has ever retained so much of his popularity so long after his best work. Tommy Handley, the best-loved comic of the Second World War, now sounds old-fashioned and difficult to understand; the other top radio and television comics of the 1950s now sound singularly dated (with the one exception of the Goons, who served a rather specialized cult market); and even the top comics of the 1970s, Morecambe and Wise, seem unlikely to retain quite the aura of Hancock.

Hancock was an instinctive comedian who, in collaboration with his best writers, Ray Galton and Alan Simpson, raised the more naturalistic type of broadcast comedy to entirely new heights; from his start in the Variety theatres he made a highly successful transition to radio and television, creating a character who has become a permanent part of the national consciousness. Lines from his most famous shows are still quoted in ordinary conversation — sometimes by people who are too young to have seen the original transmissions — and the repeat series already mentioned demonstrated a comic power that transcended the black-and-white and poor technical quality of the recordings, which would have lessened the effect of most performers for a modern audience.

Something of the quality of Hancock's work can be seen in the photographs presented in this book, which — though lacking the movement and sound of his performances — nevertheless convey to a surprising degree the personality of the comedian. His expressive face could speak volumes, and even in the more relaxed rehearsal and off-screen photographs the underlying and instinctive comic persona of the man is apparent. The text accompanying the photographs will explain the stories of the shows from which they come, or give the background to the pictures. However, this book is not a biography as such, nor a close study of his work — that has already been done elsewhere — and in particular it will not deal with his inner troubles or the sad final few years leading up to his suicide in 1968, when his difficulties had made him only a shadow of the man he was; it is the Hancock of his peak years, as he is best remembered today, who is presented here.

His professional career ranged from just after the war, in 1945, to his last uncompleted work in Australia in 1968; and encompassed live theatre, radio, television, and (to a lesser extent) the cinema. The character he created emerged gradually, taking its complete shape in the late 1950s — the unsuccessful, lone, self-opinionated and not over-bright loser, neatly described by Galton and Simpson as 'a shrewd, cunning, high-powered mug'. He was very much a part of the 1950s — although his appeal remains intact in a world changed almost beyond recognition.

It was in some ways an uneasy decade; although there was increasing material prosperity, and many people were living in much better circumstances than they could have hoped for before the war, the shadow of the atomic bomb and the memories of wartime coloured most of the period. Most radio comedy — and the relatively small amount of television comedy — aimed to reassure people rather than rock the boat in any way. Undemanding domestic situation comedies and predictable sketch shows abounded (again, the subversive *Goon Show* was an honourable exception) and even the best broadcast material tended to have what seems today a very cosy atmosphere.

The emergence of *Hancock's Half-Hour* as the greatest of all situation comedies did not happen overnight; but by the end of the 1950s the series, both on radio and television, achieved a quality not only of comedy but of depth of characterization which was far beyond anything of the period. Though he never played for sympathy or pathos, Hancock gained the understanding of his listeners as he railed against his own failures and the failure of life to be what he felt it should be; and Galton and Simpson's scripts reflected the underlying uncertainty of the decade instead of offering the easy reassurance of most comedy. Many people have attempted to sum up their style, but it was perhaps best described by Clive Hodgson (in the National Film Theatre's programme booklet when they showed a season of Hancock material) when he said that Galton and Simpson's scripts 'were closer to *Waiting for Godot* (change forever promised but never realized) than to conventional situation comedy (change constantly threatened, but always avoided)'.

Hancock's Half-Hour was of course his most famous vehicle, but there were also other television shows for ITV, plus two major and three minor film appearances; and in this pictorial celebration glimpses of these as well as some of his greatest performances, and some personal photographs, are presented as a tribute to a comic who was not only the greatest of his time but whose appeal remains as fresh today.

Hancock's early years in show business paralleled those of many other performers of the period — a few amateur appearances, call-up into the Army or Air Force during the Second World War leading to various appearances in troop entertainments, and then the post-war struggle to find work in the competitive world of theatrical Variety. In Hancock's case his experience in the RAF Gang Shows, with other young hopefuls such as Peter Sellers, Robert Moreton and Graham Stark, provided invaluable experience, and led to a tour with Ralph Reader's forces show *Wings* some six months after his demobilization.

After playing one of the Ugly Sisters in *Cinderella* at the Oxford Playhouse, he appeared with Derek Scott at the Windmill Theatre. Here, with Scott as his accompanist, he presented what would become the core of his stage act — the impression of a tatty end-of-the-pier concert party, in which he played all the performers. It was here that he developed the impressions which surfaced from time to time in his TV work — Charles Laughton in *Mutiny on the Bounty* and *The Hunchback of Notre Dame*, George Arliss (a once-famous English actor in Hollywood films who by this time was already dead), and, added later on, Robert Newton's over-the-top version of Long John Silver. As imitations, they were rather bad, although many critics have missed the point that this was entirely deliberate. Even when introduced into the TV shows they were intended to suggest that Hancock was a far from successful impersonator (despite the character's own impressions to the contrary) and in the stage appearances it was their awfulness that made them so funny — the Robert Newton one in particular, as

Hancock balanced uncertainly on one leg ('How these storks keep this up all day I'll never know') rolling his eyes and addressing imprecations to an imaginary parrot on his shoulder ('I cannot aboide that bird, most birds I can aboide but that bird I cannot aboide').

From the Windmill he went on to tour in Variety for several years — by himself but with basically the same act — but it was not until March 1952 that he reached his full potential as a stage performer, in the revue *London Laughs* at the Adelphi Theatre. By this time he had become well known on radio, in *Educating Archie*; and in *London Laughs* he worked with another well-established radio comedian, the boisterous Jimmy Edwards. Hancock and Edwards were complete opposites in their comic technique — Edwards was outgoing and self-confident as a performer, and would happily ad-lib and harangue the audience. Hancock, on the other hand, was incapable of ad-libbing, and would react to Edwards by simply doing nothing — which, rather to Hancock's bemusement, would get even louder laughs.

Despite his success in this show — and its similar successor, *The Talk of the Town* (also with Jimmy Edwards), Hancock was never really happy on stage. Eric Sykes, who wrote *Educating Archie* and was a good friend of Hancock's, comments: 'I helped him with some of his material, which he enjoyed, but in actual fact he hated the stage — I think it was because he never knew what it was that made people laugh. Not knowing is a great uncertainty — less talented people can bounce on a stage and belt something out, and they have no fear ... but Tony always had fears because he didn't know. It's only the good people who don't know, and therefore become more vulnerable. He felt that he wasn't really a stage performer.'

Talk of the Town, which opened in June 1954, included two famous sketches featuring Hancock; in the lighthouse keeper sketch 'Send in the Relief,' written by Frank Muir and Denis Norden from an original sketch by Michael Bentine, he and Edwards argued and indulged in slapstick — every time Hancock opened the door to check the weather he got a faceful of water and fish; and in 'The Crooner' he satirized pop performers such as Johnny Ray and Frank Sinatra. This sketch, written by Ray Galton and Alan Simpson (who were now writing his radio material) became the best part of his regular stage act. ('How Frank Sinatra does an hour and a half in these boots I'll never know. I've got toes like globe artichokes. It's a pleasure to get off one foot onto the other.')

Dennis Main Wilson, the producer of Hancock's early radio series, used to visit Hancock behind the scenes, and remembers: 'I'd listen on the Tannoy in his dressing-room, and he'd do 'The Crooner' or the lighthouse keeper sketch — and the laughs never came in the same place twice … and he'd come in, and I'd say, "What did you do on the so-and-so line? — it's a straight line, and you stopped the show with it!" — "Did I?" … he honestly didn't know. His performance was intuitive, rather than cerebral, and this I think is the total clue to Hancock.'

Talk of the Town placed a considerable strain on Hancock, and after he left the show his dislike of stage and the pressures of his TV work prevented him making many more stage appearances. He toured occasionally with his own show, appearing in a number of sketches in the second half (the first half being supporting acts). In his opening routine he argued with the band-leader about the speed of his walk-on music, and then complained to the audience about his difficulties in getting to the theatre: 'I wore out four pairs of shoes. Terrible time I had, sticking me hand out at passing cars — didn't get a single lift and I had four pairs of gloves whipped.'

His other routines included an attempt to recite the speech before Harfleur from *Henry V* in a park setting — with interruptions from a tramp; and a tailor's shop sketch in which he got a customer to lie down on a sheet of cloth with his arms and legs stretched out, and then drew a line round him, shouting offstage: 'Cut out two of these and sew 'em together'.

Despite his dislike of stage work — which often made him feel physically ill — he was an extremely effective performer; the intimacy of the radio and TV performances which are now so well remembered gives little hint of his power on stage; even in the largest theatre he could dominate the audience.

He played two Royal Variety performances — in 1952 and 1958 — making a considerable impression each time on that most difficult of audiences; and when he toured in the early 1960s with his show he drew large and enthusiastic audiences. The affection of audiences for him was an important part of his appeal, and even in the 1966 appearance at the Royal Festival Hall (mounted by BBC Television for a subsequent transmission) the warmth of the audience — who seemed to be almost willing him to succeed — almost overcame the effects that his personal difficulties were by this time having on his performance. For those in the hall this appearance was a success — it was only through the clinical eye of the TV camera that the performance was revealed as a shadow of his former appearances. The RFH is, of course, an almost impossibly difficult venue for a comedian, and the fact that a section of the audience was behind him, in the choir seats, only made things more difficult. In his opening remarks he commented: 'Always bothers me a bit when the audience is behind you. Seems to bring in a strange sort of person. Any case, I don't like these places where there's no smoking and coffee and Tchaikovsky in the interval.'

Had Hancock been able to come to terms with the particular strains of live performance he might perhaps have been one of the greatest stage comedians of the time — certainly on a par with the superb Sid Field, whom Hancock greatly admired and who, for other reasons, also never fully realized his potential. Even so, Hancock's stage performances were those of a marvellously talented and brilliantly funny comedian, and even though his abilities found a more suitable outlet in radio and television, his stage appearances were an important and rewarding part of his career.

RIGHT:
An almost unrecognizably young Hancock at the very start of his career.

ABOVE:
Hancock in a self-consciously funny pose; only gradually did he work towards the character who was completely unaware that he was being funny.

RIGHT:
Hancock displaying two of the obvious trappings of the inexperienced comic — the funny face and the funny hat. As time went on his development as a comic led him to discard all the props — not only easy visual tricks but also actual jokes as such — as he worked towards a character whose humour lay in his natural reactions to the realistic situations around him.

ABOVE:
In 1950 Hancock married Cicely Romanis. Here they are seen disembarking from Hancock's prized boat — a converted army pontoon.

TOP RIGHT:
Hancock (right) with John Moffat as the Ugly Sisters in Hancock's first pantomime, Cinderella, *at the Playhouse Theatre, Oxford, December 1947. It was apparently a very intellectual panto, with people chatting about Nietzsche in the ballroom scene.*

BOTTOM RIGHT:
Hancock appeared in only three pantomimes; he hated the medium, and in particular he hated having to lead the audience participation songs such as 'Every Little Piggy has a Curly Tail', which he had to sing in his character as 'Jolly Jenkins' in Little Red Riding Hood *at the Theatre Royal, Nottingham, in 1951.*

ABOVE:
London Laughs (1952). *In the days before television was widespread, BBC radio used to make periodic outside broadcasts from popular West End shows, with a commentator to explain what was going on where necessary. In the Muir and Norden sketch 'A Seat in the Circle' Hancock is the luckless BBC commentator who is obstructed by Jimmy Edwards.*

TOP RIGHT:
The Talk of the Town (1954). *Relaxing in the dressing room, Hancock and Jimmy Edwards give Joan Turner a music lesson.*

BOTTOM RIGHT:
The Talk of the Town. *Hancock and Jimmy Edwards in a romantic moment with Vera Lynn.*

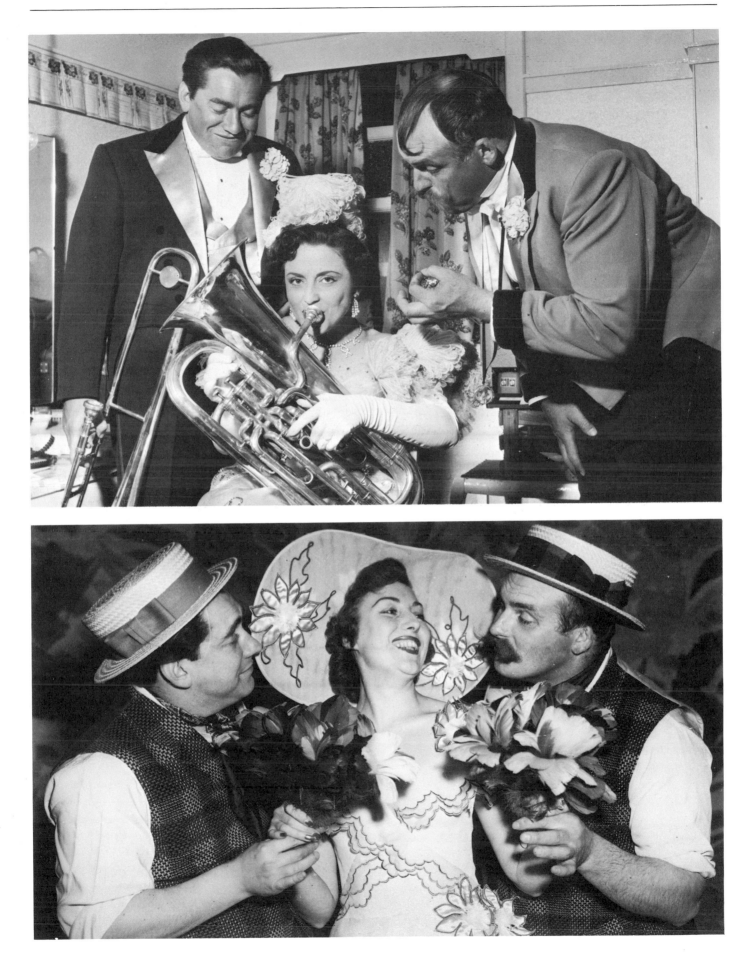

ABOVE:

The Talk of the Town. *In the lighthouse keeper sketch, 'Send the Relief,' Hancock is Edwards's assistant on a lonely lighthouse. Dedicated to keeping the light burning, they anxiously await their relief; every time Hancock opens the door to check the weather he gets a faceful of water and fish. Tension mounts; they argue and almost come to blows. In the end they are relieved by two attractive girls. Edwards: 'Shut that door — and turn that flaming light out!'*

RIGHT:

The Talk of the Town. *The lighthouse keeper sketch — Hancock checks the weather. The run of the show began in winter, and Hancock used to hate being soaked in cold water; but by the time summer arrived he looked forward to it as a relief from the high on-stage temperature.*

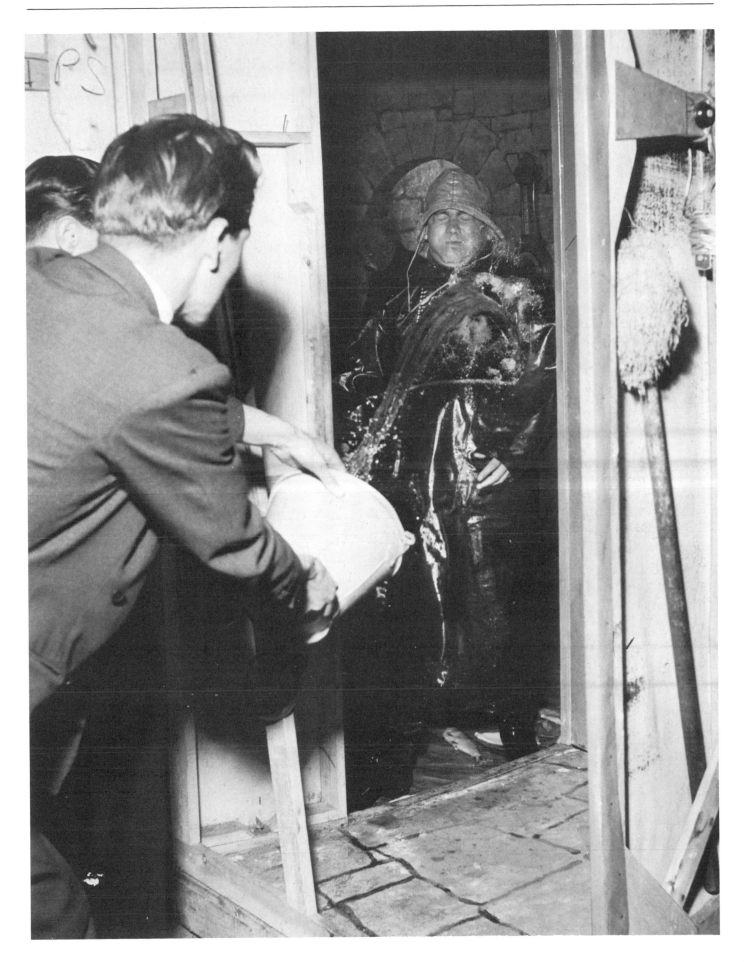

ABOVE:

The Talk of the Town. *In Hancock's 'Crooner' sketch,
written by Galton and Simpson, he is dressed in an
ill-fitting suit in a delicate pale blue — and so is his stooge.
In the argument between them, Hancock had to have his foot
stamped on every night (plus matinées); he always insisted
that the stooge must* really *stamp on him. The sketch
contained some sharp digs at the American crooners who
were then dominating the top of the bill at the Palladium.*

RIGHT:

The Talk of the Town. *At the climax of 'The Crooner'
Hancock launches into a jazzed-up version of 'Knees Up,
Mother Brown,' complete with high kicks and a good deal of
energetic movement: 'Oh, it's ridiculous. A man of my build
and calibre, leaping around like a porpoise, spending half me
life three feet off the ground. I think I'll have to get myself a
violin and a few jokes.'*

FOLLOWING PAGE:

*Hancock at the Royal Festival Hall, 22 September 1966.
Hancock performs his version of* Richard III*: 'Richard of
course was a hunchback' — an excuse for the Charles
Laughton impression yet again. At the end he does a
spectacular and protracted death scene, spoilt only by his
refusal to lie down on the stage ('not in this suit, thank
you'). In the charged atmosphere of the hall, his performance
seemed effective; this close-up photograph and the television
cameras for which the event was staged show the strain he
was working under.*

RADIO

For the first ten years or so after the war ended in 1945, radio was the major entertainment medium. Television made only slow progress, and indeed it was not until the end of the 1950s that the balance really changed in television's favour. Radio had by the end of the 1940s assumed an even greater importance than stage in the Variety world; and so it was natural that any aspiring young comic would hope to make his way on radio.

Apart from a single appearance in 1941, Hancock's radio career began in 1949 with programmes such as *Variety Bandbox*. His acts were nothing like the Hancock of the later, familiar, radio shows; he would tell unlikely stories of his experiences in monologues which were little more than a rough framework for one-line gags ('Hancock picks himself up, but after fifty yards finds himself too heavy and puts himself down again'). Gradually he developed more use of characterizations in his monologues, making less use of obtrusive gags as such; and by 1951, when he did several radio variety shows produced by Duncan Wood (who later produced the television *Hancock's Half-Hour*) he had developed considerably, as Wood remembers: 'I wouldn't ever say that he was a *good* stand-up comic; he had one or two very good acts, and when he *had* a good act and went on as second spot comic, I had one or two top comics who said to

me, "Don't book him again, because I can't follow him!" His great quality on radio was that he used to create an illusion — not telling gags, but using a number of voices — he was a character person, even then.'

His performance as tutor to Peter Brough's dummy Archie Andrews in *Educating Archie* made him famous for the first time; he appeared throughout the second series (1951), and, with the help of the writer, Eric Sykes, developed an effective comic persona. This had little resemblance to the later Hancock character, relying more upon a 'funny professor' type of voice; and it was only when he began to use material written for him by Alan Simpson and Ray Galton, in the *Star Bill* series of programmes from 1951 to 1954, that the first glimmerings of the final character could be seen. These shows — initially aimed at a forces audience and later becoming simply a high-quality Variety show — were produced in the Garrick Theatre by Dennis Main Wilson, who remembers: 'The phrase "the theatre rocked with laughter" — we used to look over the top of our equipment and literally see hundreds of shoulders heaving with laughter. This was the power of Hancock — he had the gift of making people unwind inside and laugh. Even with no line, he would fix the audience with a gimlet eye — Hancock's face, doing nothing, was conducive to enormous laughter.'

His success in these shows enabled Main Wilson and the writers to persuade the BBC that Hancock was worthy of his own series of programmes; and *Hancock's Half-Hour* began in November 1954. A good deal of thought went into creating the series. First, the writers resisted the temptation to hang the show on Hancock having any particular job. Main Wilson: 'The less detail you give to a character, the longer the show will run. Make him a Borough Councillor, for example — how many jokes are there about being a Borough Councillor? Later, I did seven series of *Till Death Us Do Part*, and to this day you don't know what Alf Garnett did for a living; and that was very carefully planned from the experience with Hancock — you never knew any detail about the character's background. The moment you start putting adjectives on a character you create a rod for your own back. Galton and Simpson, in their early twenties, had spotted that.'

A team of supporting performers was assembled: Sidney James — already well established as a Cockney character actor in films (he was in fact South African); Bill Kerr, an Australian who had been performing in Variety for several years; and, because it was traditional for comedians to have a girl-friend, Moira Lister, who played a slightly upper-class and forceful girl-friend to Hancock's rather shady and lower-class character. Kenneth Williams was in most of the first series, later joining on a regular basis, to play everyone else — policemen, judges, — in fact the voices of authority with whom Hancock could tangle.

Even in the early days, when the characterizations were not fully developed, it made a strong team. Sid James played much the same petty criminal type that he always did (although the actual criminality was later played down); Bill Kerr was Hancock's sidekick, who always knew just the man to do whatever Hancock wanted — Sid; from this would develop some complex situation which usually ended in Sid fleecing Hancock. Moria Lister's character was effective in the terms of the early shows, although as time went on the Hancock character fitted less and less well with the idea of having girl-friends.

The plots tended to be rather involved, almost cartoon-like situations — it was only gradually that the team developed the reality which was their aim. In 'The New Car' (broadcast 7 December 1954) Hancock is bemoaning the fact that he is the only radio comedian not to own a car. Bill suggests buying a second-hand one from Sid; Hancock is suspicious. 'The man's a scurrilous scalliwag.' 'Well, you said it.' 'Only just.'

Bill reassures Hancock by claiming that he is a skilled mechanic. 'I can have a car to bits in no time.'

'The way you drive that's not difficult.' However Hancock agrees to try Sid, and starts with a car of very dubious parentage. Sid: 'It's just rolled off the assembly line'. Hancock: 'Who pushed it?'. On a trial run the car turns out to be no speedster — 'Wave that tortoise on' — except down hill, when it emerges that it has no brakes.

Hancock demands a better car, and Sid sells him a swish-looking black one for £250 (Sid's mechanic is just changing the number-plates). It is only when Moira is driving it at 80 m.p.h., and Hancock notices that the police car following them is just like theirs, that he begins to be suspicious. In a panic, they hide in a field for the night — Hancock plays a romantic scene with what he thinks is Moira, but turns out to be a cow. They are then hijacked by a dangerous criminal, and a wild chase ensues. Evading the police, they deliver the criminal to his destination — Sid's used car lot — and Sid replaces the car with a big red one described as an 'open sports car'. This one turns out to be a fire engine — Hancock: 'He told me that ladder was for seeing over the top of buses!'

Moira Lister left after the first series, and was replaced for the next two series by Andrée Melly who, though effective in her own way, was again an increasingly unconvincing companion to Hancock. Otherwise the characters and situations were much the same. Much play was made with Hancock's supposed fatness and shortness — not a particularly real facet of the actual Hancock, as Alan Simpson remembers: 'He was plump — rotund — but he wasn't *fat* by any means. He was about 5ft 9in — we used a bit of licence. Bill called him "Tub" because next to Bill he *was* a bit fat, but he had one of those faces that looked fat. The *character* used to get terribly upset — "Are you insinuating that I'm portly?".'

During the second series Kenneth Williams developed one of his best-remembered characters — the little idiot with the nasal voice, whose catchphrase was 'No, stop messing about'. The character never actually had a name, and in the scripts was indicated by the instruction 'Ken (snide)', so it will be convenient to refer to him as Snide, even though the name is not a real one. One of Snide's earliest appearances is in 'The Television Set' (14 June 1955). Hancock, prepared to spend £15 on a TV set and being told by the shop that the cheapest model is £60 ('I shall buy my fuse wire elsewhere'), buys a kit from Sid and assembles it himself. It turns out to be rather bigger than expected — it occupies most of the house, and has already trapped Bill in the bathroom. However, it does work, rather surprisingly. Hancock is unimpressed by the programmes — particularly the weatherman ('Perfectly good maps, and he's chalking all over them').

Sid joins them, but just as they are settling down to watch a play Snide invites himself in: 'Oh dear — you ain't bought one of *those* sets, have you? Three weeks and you'll need a new tube.' At the exciting end of the play the set breaks down; Snide, of course is an expert ('Your timebase is tilted') and gets inside it before Hancock can stop him ('Come out! I know you're in there, I can see your face on the screen.'). In the end the set catches fire and burns the house down — one of several occasions on which a similar occurrence happens, but week-to-week consistency never really mattered.

By the end of the third series — after which Andrée Melly left — the characters had settled to more or less their final versions. Hancock had relaxed into his part, and was no longer using the self-consciously funny voice; but the greatest change was in Bill. Alan Simpson: 'Bill's character completely changed; our first conception of him was as a fast-talking American-type Australian — but a bit uncouth to give the other contrast to Hancock — but it became funnier when he became a complete idiot, like Stan Laurel ... which didn't happen overnight, it was gradual.'

Just as the characters were becoming more real, so were the situations. Instead of the unconvincing girl-friends, Hattie Jacques joined the cast to play Miss Pugh, Hancock's aggressive and overbearing secretary — a superb foil to him. Some of the plots were still rooted in impossible happenings. In 'Michelangelo 'Ancock' (18 November 1956) he decides to enter a sculpting competition, despite the requirement that the statue must be 10 ft high. Bill: 'Where are we going to find a 10 ft model?' Sid undertakes to supply the stone — which he gets by dismantling Waterloo Bridge and Nelson's Column. Hancock wins the competition, but when the statue is unveiled it draws protests from the crowd: 'It's in the nude!' Hancock: 'So would you be if you didn't have any clothes on'. Then Snide appears as the Chairman of the local Watch Committee — and also the local cinema censor ('All the bits of film I order to be cut out, I put 'em in my pocket, stick 'em together, and make one big film out of 'em. It's smashing — the plot's not very good, but, cor ...'.) He orders the statue to be destroyed; undeterred, Hancock begins work on another. But, Sid has over-reached himself and Hancock is brought before the court — 'I had no idea it was Stonehenge!' — and ends up in jail, breaking up rocks.

These physical impossibilities were beginning to jar with the reality of the programme — a problem which Simpson and Galton increasingly solved by the use of dream or fantasy sequences, as in the famous show 'The Diary' (30 December 1956), when Hancock imagines himself as, among other things, a test pilot. Even in the air he is not safe from Snide — 'I say, it ain't 'alf cold out 'ere, can I come in?' — who, once in, succeeds in ejecting both himself and Hancock out onto the tail of the plane.

Dennis Main Wilson produced the first four series of *Hancock's Half-Hour* (after which he left to work in television and was replaced by Tom Ronald) and saw the development of the character from the early seedy, semi-criminal type to the fuller, more rounded character who managed to remain completely likeable in spite of all his faults: 'He was a liar, a coward, he ducked responsibility, he was gullible, he was an arrant snob — all the things that are inherent in all of us. The beauty of it was that you could identify him not with yourself, but with your Uncle Fred or your next-door-neighbour. Johnny Speight gave those characteristics to Alf Garnett, but much more harshly, much more cruelly, in a much later, crueller world. We did the Hancock shows in a much happier world.'

With the fifth series, in 1958, the transition to the more rounded-out character was complete — aided by the television version of *Hancock's Half-Hour*, which, since TV necessarily demanded greater reality, tended to reflect this reality back into the radio shows. In this series he variously ran up against a scandal magazine run by Sid, discovered an unexploded wartime bomb in his cellar, stood for Parliament as a Liberal candidate (result: Anthony Hancock — 1), was the victim of a spate of threatening letters, and attempted to go round the world in eighty days — despite Bill's distrust of aeroplanes ('If we'd have been meant to fly they'd have given us wings, that's what I think.' Hancock: 'If you'd have been meant to think you'd have been given a brain').

The fantasy element emerged only once — in the pack of lies Hancock tells the local vicar about his wartime exploits. These include himself, Bill and Sid being the only prisoners in a German prisoner-of-war camp. Bill's escape plan is based on the 'Albert R.N.' idea — a dummy to replace an escaped prisoner during the return to the camp after exercise. Hancock: 'You ace buffoon! If there's two of us left and one dummy, that means for the next one to escape we've got to make another dummy. And when the third one gets away we're going to have three dummies helping each other in and out of the camp!'

This series also included the most famous of all his radio shows — 'Sunday Afternoon at Home' (22 April 1958) which dispensed with plot and left Hancock,

Sid, Bill and Miss Pugh staring at each other on a wet boring Sunday afternoon; the show was most notable for its use of long pauses — very daring for radio at that time. Here Hancock's timing was superb as he delayed his lines for the maximum effect.

Hancock's world of East Cheam and the dilapidated house at 23 Railway Cuttings became one of the most popular offerings on radio; as Galton and Simpson gradually eschewed the use of plot and concentrated on characterization they enabled Hancock to give a performance with a depth and warmth to it which had never before been achieved in a comedy show. The writers were by now fully familiar with the inherent qualities of the character. Ray Galton: 'Pomposity was one of the characteristics we used, especially when under attack or being questioned — he could never be deflated. And he always thought it was a good idea to meet the class of woman he desired — which would either be a scrubber or someone of high intelligence. Of course he didn't get on with either.' Alan Simpson: 'He always courted a woman in a most gentlemanly way, with the chocolates and the flowers — but cheap ones, he never spent too much, just in case. But when he did fail, he never felt sorry for himself — when the woman made it clear she didn't fancy him he always got very belligerent.'

The sixth and last radio series, at the end of 1959, pursued the lack of plot and concentration on character. Hattie Jacques left to have a baby and was not replaced; and Kenneth Williams made few appearances, since his Snide character had become out of key with the developing style of the programme. Many of the shows contain long sequences with Hancock, Sid and Bill simply arguing or discussing things, and in 'The Christmas Club' (22 December 1959), when Kerr was absent, Hancock and Sid spent about five minutes discussing whether or not to answer the door bell — another dazzling display of a technique which few other comedians could ever aspire to.

In 'Hancock in Hospital' (15 December 1959) Hancock is in traction with a broken leg, and complaining because he has had no visitors. Other people's vistors are just a nuisance: 'Look at them, pounding up the ward — anyone would think there was a sale on!' Then Sid and Bill arrive, bearing food — a packet of crisps and a pint of winkles, much to Hancock's disgust. 'Get them [the crisps] off the bed! If I get one of them down my plaster I've had it!' Boredom sets in; Sid is forbidden to smoke, and Bill finds his own way of amusing himself (Hancock: 'Stop drawing on my leg.'). When they finally leave, the nurse comes round. 'Ah, there you are, Mr Hancock.' 'Where did you expect me to be?' She takes his plaster off, but, standing up for the first time, he slips on a winkle shell and breaks the other leg — the sort of circular ending to the plot that Galton and Simpson were fond of.

The radio shows have made a continuing impact, because of relatively frequent repeats — which still continue on special occasions, even after twenty-five years — and the various complete shows and extracts available on gramophone records. There has been little advance in radio comedy since then, and no one of Hancock's stature; and today the shows still stand up as superb examples of radio comedy, miniature dramas in their own right and providing the basis of characterization to which the visual element of the television shows was added.

FOLLOWING PAGES: LEFT
Educating Archie. *Hancock with Hattie Jacques, who played Agatha Dinglebody in the series; she was later to be an excellent foil for him in* Hancock's Half-Hour.

RIGHT:
Educating Archie. *Hancock as Archie's tutor. The scripts were by Eric Sykes and Sid Colin. Sykes in particular worked with Hancock on creating his first important persona — the pompous, irascible, and slow-witted 'funny professor' type which Hancock gradually refined during his subsequent radio appearances until he began to find the final version of the character which saw him through six years of* Hancock's Half-Hour.

Educating Archie. *Hancock with Peter Brough and Archie.
Hancock's appearances as Archie's tutor in the 1951 series
gave him his first big break. He played two characters — the
other, who could have various jobs to suit the situation, gave
him his first catchphrase — 'flippin' kids!'. Here, in his
character as Archie's tutor he was able to allow his
pomposity full play. He never much cared for the show,
though, and the sight of the dummy hung up on a hook in
Peter Brough's dressing room used to give him nightmares
for years.*

LEFT:
This photograph, which neatly captures the essence of Hancock's character as Archie Andrews' tutor, was taken by Graham Stark, who was a keen amateur photographer as well as an effective comic who appeared as support to Hancock in the Happy-Go-Lucky and Star Bill radio programmes.

ABOVE:
Star Bill (1954). Hancock, Moira Lister and Graham Stark were a regular team on this series of the hour-long variety show. They appeared in sketches, written by Galton and Simpson, which to some extent pre-figured the Hancock's Half-Hour domestic set-up, and indeed Moira Lister was carried over to the first series. Stark, though a good foil to Hancock, had rather too similar a voice at that time, which may have been why he was replaced by Bill Kerr. Here they strike a pose for the publicity photographer.

LEFT:
A very young-looking Alan Simpson (left) and Ray Galton pose with Hancock. During the Forces All-Star Bill *and* Star Bill *variety programmes between 1952 and 1954 in which Hancock used their scripts they began to build the complex Hancock radio personality, making use of his particular abilities in a very perceptive way. Though not up to the more mature* Hancock's Half-Hours, *their sketches for* Star Bill *are well written and amusing.*

FOLLOWING PAGES:
The Hancock persona of the Star Bill *programmes was something of a fly boy, exhibiting a petty criminality which only later gave way to the seedy gentility of the character in his own radio series. This sequence of three photographs demonstrates something of the early 1950s Hancock character, by turns unctuous, bombastic, and displaying touches of that departed phenomenon of the period, the spiv.*

This 1954 portrait by Baron seems to suggest Hancock's
inner worries which at that time were well below the surface.

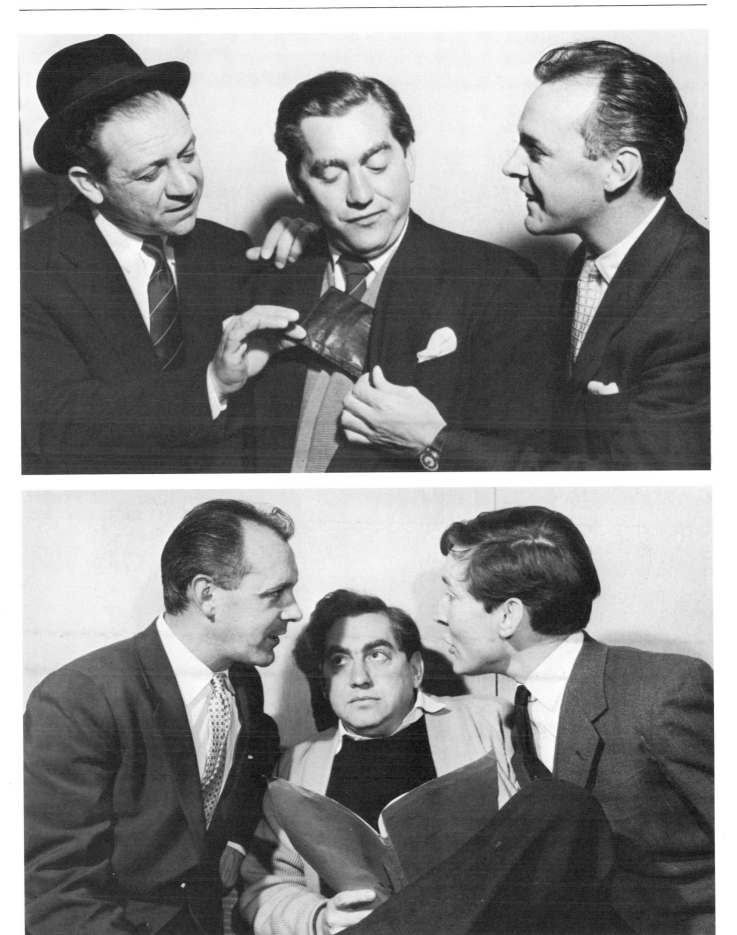

RIGHT:
Sidney James, Hancock and Bill Kerr pose for a publicity photograph for the beginning of the first series of Hancock's Half-Hour *in 1954.*

PREVIOUS PAGES — TOP LEFT:
With his increasing fame — and therefore income — Hancock could afford an expensive car. However, he was never much of a driver, and Cicely did most of the driving. Here they study a road map for the benefit of a press photographer.

BOTTOM LEFT:
Hancock's Half-Hour. *1954: with his own series at last, Hancock and the writers could develop the characters in much greater detail. In the early shows, Bill Kerr (right) was much more sharp-witted than he later became, while Hancock was still making use of his tight-throated funny voice. Here he appears to be rejecting another of Bill's bright ideas — probably one involving Sid James.*

TOP RIGHT:
Having chosen Bill Kerr as a sidekick for Hancock, Galton and Simpson were looking for a good foil for him. They saw just the person they wanted in the film The Lavender Hill Mob, *and had to see the film round again to find out who it was — Sidney James (on the left in the picture), already well established in Cockney character parts, particularly taxi-drivers and petty criminals. In* Hancock's Half-Hour *he always had some complicated scheme which ended up with Hancock much the poorer, if no wiser.*

BOTTOM RIGHT:
Kenneth Williams (right) was brought in by the producer, Dennis Main Wilson, to act the various voices of authority with whom Hancock could argue — policemen, judges, petty officials and so on. He also played Sid's criminal accomplice, Edwardian Fred, and, later, the 'Snide' character who became so well known.

ABOVE:
Hancock's Half-Hour. *A publicity pose for 'The Monte Carlo Rally' (18 January 1955). Hancock has entered the rally, in a car supplied by Sid — dating from 1896. Difficulties abound: Hancock has a discussion in French with a Customs inspector. Bill: 'What did he say?' Hancock: 'Never mind about him — what did I say?'. The weather turns treacherous — the snow is a foot deep inside the car. In the end, it turns out to have been a dream. Hancock wakes up to find that he is stuck on the starting-line, and has collected a parking-ticket.*

RIGHT:
A 1956 publicity portrait.

Sid practises his manual skills while Hancock discusses something with Bill Kerr.

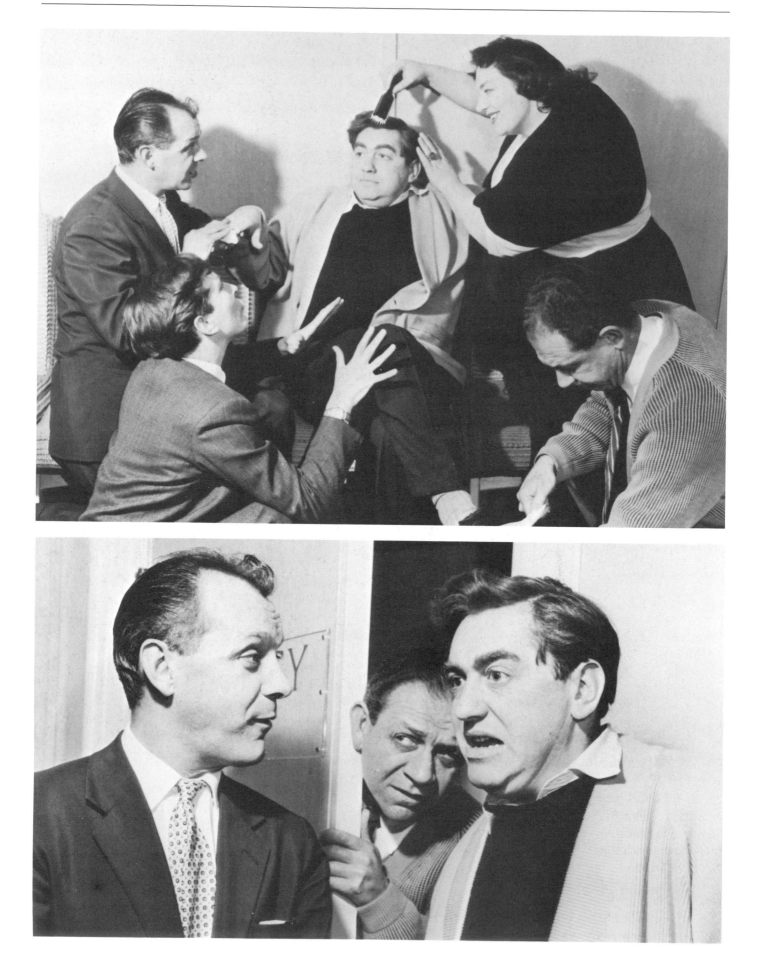

TOP LEFT:
Hancock receives the attentions which are only proper to a man of his calibre. Bill Kerr, Kenneth Williams and Sidney James are joined by Hattie Jacques — who looks rather too friendly for her character of Hancock's aggressive secretary, Grizelda Pugh.

BOTTOM LEFT:
Hancock protests, Bill can't see what there is to worry about, and Sid has an eye on the main chance.

ABOVE:
Hancock hides behind Alan Simpson (left) and Ray Galton. Hancock was not as short as he looks here — but then Simpson and Galton are very tall.

LEFT:
Hancock poses in musical vein.

FOLLOWING PAGE — TOP:
One of the best-known publicity photographs. Kenneth Williams watches relaxedly while Hancock scores a point off an increasingly dim-witted Bill Kerr. Sid James looks as down-to-earth as always.

BOTTOM:
Hancock clowns with Hattie Jacques during rehearsals.

BBC TELEVISION

Hancock made a few odd appearances on television in his early days, but then his work on radio kept him off TV until 1955. His first television series was not for the BBC, but, because of an involved contractual situation arising out of his stage work, was produced by Jack Hylton and transmitted on ITV; this will be covered briefly in the next section, dealing with Hancock's ITV work.

With his contractual obligations to Hylton out of the way, Hancock — who was by now well established on radio — began his BBC Television version of *Hancock's Half-Hour*. The first series was transmitted in 1956, and the second early the following year. In its early stages the show was still very verbal — both the writers and Hancock had to learn to use the new medium. Galton and Simpson took the decision not to try to carry the complete *menage* from 23 Railway Cuttings over to television — it would simply have presented them with too many characters to cope with on a regular basis, particularly as television tends to move more slowly than radio. Bill Kerr was dropped, and Kenneth Williams and Hattie Jacques made only a few appearances. Sid James made an ideal foil for Hancock on television — he was already well established in the cinema, and so had more experience than the rest of the team in working

visually; he was able to teach Hancock a lot about using the new medium properly.

The producer was Duncan Wood, who, together with designer Roy Oxley, carefully worked out the set of 23 Railway Cuttings which was, with minor variations, to last until the sixth series. He rapidly established a good working relationship with Hancock, who found the new medium something of a strain, particularly since, unlike in radio, he had to learn a complete half-hour script every week.

With the third series, which began in September 1957, the team were well into their stride, and the series contains a number of very good shows. The supporting casts were of course much larger than on radio, and featured a number of well-known comic actors on a fairly regular basis, among them Arthur Mullard, John Le Mesurier, John Vere, Alec Bregonzi, Hugh Lloyd, Mario Fabrizi and the dimunitive Johnny Vyvyan. Though the situations were less unreal than in the early radio shows, there was still an atmosphere of a comedy show rather than the naturalistic feel that the team later worked towards, so the fact that the same performers turned up week after week in different roles was not distracting in a way which would apply if the same technique were used in *Yes, Minister* or *To the Manor Born*.

Not all the shows by any means concentrated on 23 Railway Cuttings. In 'The Lawyer — The Crown v. James S. — Hancock QC Defending' (2 December 1957) Hancock is a barrister — albeit one with the mannerisms rather than the actual abilities of a QC. In the first scene a long-distance lorry driver is on trial for bigamy — eight times. Hancock makes a splendidly dramatic prosecuting speech, and the prisoner is sentenced to six years. There is only one snag — Hancock was supposed to be defending him. When he gets back to chambers his employing barrister catalogues the mess Hancock has already made of ten other cases, particularly the last: 'An important murder case and you turn up in the wrong court — you spend three hours making an impassioned plea for a life sentence on a man accused of passing betting-slips in Hyde Park!'

Against his better judgement, the barrister gives Hancock one last chance, defending one of their regular clients — it is, of course, Sid James. Visiting Sid in the police station Hancock falls foul of the desk sergeant and is given a succession of tickets for various offences with his car — he ends up in the same cell as Sid. At the trial, Sid tosses a coin to determine his plea — not guilty — and relates how he was looking in a window in Bond Street when he was shoved aside and someone else threw a brick through the window — Sid was trying to put the jewelry *back* when the police arrived. In the last scene we see Hancock in Dartmoor — Sid has identified *him* as the man who threw the brick.

All these programmes were broadcast 'live' — a considerable strain on everyone involved, since nothing could be done if something went wrong. In 'There's an Airfield at the Bottom of my Garden' (16 December 1957) something *did* go wrong — a collapsible set developed a will of its own and for about five minutes Hancock and the others were struggling to fit their lines into a changing situation — and as a result half the next series and all the subsequent shows were pre-recorded, the later ones on the new videotape system. This also helped to overcome Hancock's occasional habit of fluffing by replacing the words with ones which had the same rhythm but a completely different meaning — 'Who's been messing about with my concrete toadstools?' in a garden sequence came out as 'Who's been messing about with my cardboard nutmegs?'.

Hancock had to find ways of helping with his difficulty in learning lines; one way was using a tape recorder, and another was bolstering his memory by having lines written on bits of paper at strategic points on the set. Hugh Lloyd was in the fourth series

show 'The Oak Tree' (13 March 1959) in which Johnny Vyvyan was one of a group of professional protest marchers Hancock had hired. Lloyd remembers: 'There was a scene in a garden where there were plants with labels on, and Tony had some of his lines written on the labels; then we played a joke on him. Johnny Vyvyan had to show the soles of his shoes to prove that they've been worn out [by marching], and we chalked Tony's next line on the sole of the shoe. It absolutely corpsed him — he was well capable of laughing at himself in those days.'

Hancock's characteristics were carried over intact from the radio shows — including snobbery, as evidenced by his desire for recognition in 'The Knighthood' (20 March 1959). At the start of the show his dreams of grandeur have led him to force Sid to act as his butler. ('You don't come in here and say "What do you want?" — you say "You rang, sir?"'; Sid: 'I *know* you rang, it's up on the board — what do you want?') Hancock feels he has been passed over — 'Alec Guinness got a knighthood, why shouldn't I?'. Persuaded by Sid that television comics never get knighthoods, Hancock tries to bluff his way into the Old Vic — 'Kindly tell Old Vic I'm here'. He gets a glimpse of Sir Ralph Richardson's contract — 'Is that all he's getting?'. After a demonstration of his method of playing Hamlet in the style of Robert Newton (as Long John Silver) he is told to join a repertory company to gain experience. He manages to do so, and we see him briefly as Mark Antony, Richard III, and Romeo — all complete with crutch and parrot ('But soft, what light through yonder window breaks — ha harr . . .'). He finally does get a job at the Old Vic — as prompter.

The developing Hancock persona included, as we have already seen, faults that should have combined to make him a very unlikeable person. It was a tribute both to the writers and to Hancock himself that he remained sympathetic. Duncan Wood: 'The character was a fool, basically, but you had great sympathy with him — that marvellously mobile face, coupled with the voice, produced a likeable character no matter what he did or said; he looked like a beaten-up spaniel — even if the dog bites you you still pat it on the head again.'

Hancock's use of his face was one of the major comic assets of the show. Several expressions could chase over it in the few seconds before a line so that his thought processes were quite apparent — none of this was in the script, and it was entirely instinctive; Hancock never really knew consciously what he was doing, but the effect was always hilarious and added a whole new dimension to the already excellent scripts.

The scripts themselves were developing to a very high standard as Galton and Simpson learned how to make the best use of television. Hugh Lloyd remembers: 'There were more things cut than were added during the rehearsals, and this is where Tony and Alan and Ray were very clever, because anything that seemed like a joke, on its own grounds, was left out — whether or not we hooted at it — because unless it was true to the story and the character it used to be turned out'.

One of the principal techniques Hancock had developed was that of facial reaction to other people's remarks and actions. Hugh Lloyd: 'Whereas once upon a time comics used to say, "I want the funny lines", Tony realized that in television it didn't matter who had the comedy lines provided you cut to him for the reaction'. By reacting to an already funny line — showing for example that he thought the speaker was an idiot — he could cap it, and thus get two laughs on one line. This technique complicated Duncan Wood's job, since much more rapid camera cutting was necessary than had been normal in comedy shows up to then.

With the fifth series, which began in September 1959, the shows were for the first time sold to foreign TV stations — particularly in Australia, where they developed a considerable following. From the beginning of this series until the end of Hancock's BBC TV work all the shows still exist, and every one of them is a classic of comedy; despite the muddy quality of the prints (the original videotapes having been destroyed) and the occasional technical rough edges, they stand up today as well as they ever did.

As with the radio shows, there was more dependence on character and less on plot; much of the comedy came from the interplay of Hancock and Sid, and Hancock's attempts to come to terms with the unsympathetic world outside. In 'The Economy Drive' (25 September 1959) Hancock embarks on an attempt to save money wasted by Sid leaving everything in the house running while they were on holiday; in 'The Two Murderers' (2 October 1959) each of them thinks the other is out to murder him for his money; and in 'Twelve Angry Men' (16 October 1959) Hancock, as foreman of a jury, attempts to emulate Henry Fonda's feat of persuading all the remaining jurors to change their verdict.

The Hancock character, of course, always fancied himself with the women — although Sid, who aimed lower, always had more success. In 'The Big Night' (6 November 1959) the two of them begin by spending a Saturday morning planning the evening ahead. Sid is going to dress up to the nines: 'Clean dicky dirt, new

Peckham, pair of luminous almond rocks, new whistle, nice crease in me strides, barnet well greased up, and flashing me 'ampsteads at all the bona pallones'. Hancock: 'I didn't understand a single word you said, but it sounds marvellous'. Hancock's housekeeper, the awful Mrs Cravatte (a magnificent creation by Patricia Hayes) brings in an unappetising breakfast — oeufs scrambléd. 'But it's Saturday — it's a special day — can't you do something special for breakfast?' 'That *is* special — you wait 'till you see what you're getting on Monday.'

Discovering that Mrs Cravatte has failed to wash their shirts they venture to the local launderette — a new experience for Hancock, who has never seen an automatic washing machine: 'Isn't that marvellous! When I think of my poor old mother on the banks of the canal with those two great big stones!' Sid has pinched Hancock's soap powder: 'You're trying to make your shirt look whiter than mine, so that when you come and stand by me people will start singing about me mother'.

However, the machine tears Hancock's shirt to ribbons, so he has to turn up at the cinema that evening dressed as a beatnik — polo-neck sweater and beret. They fail to pick up any girls outside so Sid suggests trying inside: 'There might be a bit of spare stuff floating around in there — and with the lights down you won't be so much of a lumber. All you've got to do now is, you get 'em as soon as they come through the curtains and they can't see what they're doing.'

They find seats, and Sid spots a couple of girls in front of them (Sid: 'I don't fancy yours'). They move in, but the girls promptly get up and leave. They split up to hunt on their own, and we next see them being booted out of the cinema. Hancock is outraged: 'How dare you manhandle me like that? We only sat next to her to talk to her — I didn't know she was the organist! We were just as surprised as you were when we all shot up in the air!'

In desperation they try to get themselves arrested by a couple of policewomen, only to be picked up by two policemen. 'We want to be arrested by those two young ladies over there.' Policeman: 'Oh yes? — well, that's my missus!' Hancock knocks the policeman's helmet off: 'That should take care of next Saturday as well'.

The fantasy element of the early radio or one or two of the early TV shows was now almost completely absent. In 'The Tycoon' (13 November 1959) a fantasy sequence was fitted in, under the usual guise of a dream. Hancock, sleeping through a shareholder's meeting of the East Cheam Building

Society, dreams that he is a tycoon who owns half the world — the other half being owned by Aristotle Thermopylae. They agree to a game of cards to decide who shall own *all* the world — but Sid joins in and persuades them to play 'Chinaman's Whist'. Sid: 'All twos, sevens and nines are wild, except if you have the three of hearts with the jack of clubs in which case diamonds are trumps. It must be played three-handed, and the third player has the privilege of sitting in without having to put up a stake.' Sid, of course, is the third player. He is also the dealer, because he is sitting on the left of the one owning the pack of cards. On the first deal, it turns out that the lowest card (Sid's) is the winner. On the second deal, Sid changes the rules so that it is only on the first deal that the lowest card wins ... and so on. Needless to say, Sid wins everything. Hancock: 'Even in me dreams he's still at it!'

During all this time, Hancock was finding television a tremendous strain, even though he still preferred having to perform a new story each week to having to keep repeating himself week after week in the theatre. The mechanical difficulties of learning lines were only one problem; he was beginning to try to understand how it was that he could be so funny without really knowing why — an ill-advised train of thought, which was not helped by his appearance in the interview series *Face to Face*, in which John Freeman subjected well-known personalities to intensive personal questioning. Even so, his performances were not visibly affected, and the sixth series — his last with Sid James — set an extremely high standard throughout. In some of the shows the humour was drawn from very simple situations; for example in 'The Missing Page' (11 March 1960) he tried to track down the missing last page of a crime thriller, and in 'The Baby-Sitters' (8 April 1960) he and Sid made the most unlikely pair of baby-sitters ever seen.

Many of the shows gave him opportunities for extraordinary displays of comic technique. In 'The Reunion Party' (25 March 1960) he and Sid hold a party for a group of Hancock's wartime comrades. Of course after fifteen years, they have nothing in common and little to say to each other — which enabled Hancock to make good use of pauses, as Duncan Wood remembers: 'The conversation would run for about three seconds, and then a long pause — and Hancock had the line which took them out of that pause, so he had total control of the pace of that show. Nobody else could do anything until he spoke — and as a total comprehensive demonstration of how to control the length of a pause before it goes over the edge — I can't think of anyone else who

could have done it.' This show also includes a sequence where Hancock spends all of 45 seconds (which is a longer time than it sounds) doing nothing more than trying unsuccessfully to remember someone's name.

Hancock's pretensions to respectability lead him into local government in 'The East Cheam Centenary' (29 April 1960) which begins with a long sequence — without Sid — in which the local Council attempts to make plans to celebrate the centenary. The rest of the councillors seem to be about Hancock's level of efficiency. An elderly councillor suggests sending the old people to Brighton for the day. Hancock: 'He always suggests that — just because he's the only one that's entitled to go'. Hancock suggests doing up all the houses in the borough — which he always suggests because his is the only one that needs doing up. The Mayor suggests a souvenir edition of the East Cheam Gazette. Hancock: 'This will set the whole world buzzing with complete disinterest. How can you have a souvenir edition of a thing that only sells 450 copies, and most of that to the local fish shop?' A row ensues, with accusations and counter-accusations in which it emerges that Hancock's post on the Cottage Hospital committee is keeping him in orange juice for his parties.

Another councillor (Hugh Lloyd) suggests a battle of flowers — an idea no one of the Council has ever heard of. Lloyd explains that he saw one on holiday in the South of France: 'They threw some at me!' Hancock: 'I don't blame them! They must have left one of the pots on!' This leads on to an altercation with another councillor about the lack of flowers on the floral clock in the park — and works beneath them for that matter: 'Those hands haven't moved for four years — it's been four buttercups past milkweed since 1956.'

Eventually they settle on a carnival, and Hancock goes home to plan it. One of the vehicles is a lorry for people to throw money into for charity. Sid: 'Who's driving that?' Hancock: 'You're not! It's your idea of paradise, isn't it — a load of loot and a getaway car all in one'. With the plans laid, Sid and Hancock sell the TV coverage rights to the BBC; unfortunately for them the Major has sold the rights to ITV, so Hancock and Sid have to mount their own extremely tatty procession — with a TV commentary provided by an increasingly bemused John Snagge.

The popularity of *Hancock's Half-Hour* was by this time enormous — Alan Simpson remembers fish-and-chip shops complaining to the BBC that they had no customers for half-an-hour every Friday night. Hancock however was growing unhappy, particularly over the whole milieu of 23 Railway Cuttings, the relationship with Sid, and his frequent costume of the homburg hat and the coat with the astrakhan collar. He felt that he had pushed this combination as far as it could go and also he had a desire to increase the social standing of his character slightly — partly on the grounds that the fall from a greater height would be funnier. After considerable heart-searching and discussion by all concerned it was decided to drop Sid James from the next series, and to find a different background for what would be basically the same Hancock character. The last show of the sixth series, 'The Poison Pen Letters' (6 May 1960) — his last appearance with Sid James — provided an excuse for the change of address. Hancock is very disturbed by some poison pen letters he has been receiving. After getting little help from the police, it eventually emerges that Hancock has been writing them himself — in his sleep. As Sid points out: 'You're just like everybody else, really — *you* don't like you either!' Hancock decides to take evasive action: 'I'll move, that's it — I'll change me address, then me subconscious won't know where to look for me'.

Before his seventh and last BBC TV series Hancock made the cinema film *The Rebel*, which will be dealt with in a later section. It formed part of his hopes for international recognition; and for the same reason the TV programmes were now reduced to a 25-minute slot, in the hope (which remained unfulfilled) that they might be sold to America (the five minutes allowing time for commercials). Re-named simply *Hancock*, the shows were now based round a bed-sitting room in Earl's Court; in fact the first show, 'The Bedsitter' (26 May 1961 — also sometimes known as 'Hancock Alone') was set entirely in the bedsitter and had no supporting actors.

The programme was a considerable *tour de force*, and extremely successful. Hancock simply wandered around the flat talking to himself — attempting to cope with a difficult book, trying to make the television work, attempting (unsuccessfully) to chat up girls on the phone ('Leopard-skin tights — at her age!'). At one point he examines his teeth in a mirror: 'Is that loose? — or is it me fingers going in and out?'. He muses on the meaning of the word 'bicuspid', trying various possible uses, as in 'By Cuspid, he's a handsome fellow, Sir Charles'. Ray Galton: 'He launched into a piece of mime of a dandy taking snuff, bowing, parrying swords — it was a perfect few seconds of movement. I was amazed at the beauty of it — observation, just observation'. Alan Simpson adds: 'It was almost as if it had been choreographed'.

It is the shows in this series which are the best remembered: 'The Lift', 'The Radio Ham' (both later

released in new performances for gramophone records) and the hilarious dig at BBC radio's rural soap-opera *The Archers* in 'The Bowmans' in which he gave a devastating impression of Walter Gabriel. Most famous of course is 'The Blood Donor' (23 June 1961), again largely because of its gramophone record performance (although this show did get one repeat during the sixteen-year drought of Hancock on television). The difficult circumstances under which this show was made are now well known: the car accident the week before which prevented Hancock being able to learn the script, and the reliance on autocue and prompt cards adversely affected Hancock's performance. Nevertheless the script is a classic, beautifully constructed — complete with a typical Galton and Simpson circular ending in which Hancock, having injured himself, has to be given a transfusion of the blood he has only recently given.

It was never intended at the time that the seventh series should be the last for the BBC; but difficulties between the writers and Hancock over the script for another film led to their parting company; and then Galton and Simpson went on to write *Steptoe and Son* (itself a partial re-working of the Hancock–James relationship in a different setting) while Hancock went on to make his next film, *The Punch and Judy Man* and then make a television series for ATV. By this time Hancock on the one hand and Galton and Simpson on the other were approaching their work in different ways; Hancock still trying to upgrade the character and make him internationally acceptable, and Galton and Simpson pursuing a socially downward trend into Steptoe's junkyard.

The BBC TV shows — particularly the last three series — remain among the very top television comedies ever made. The team had progressed from more traditional forms of comedy to what in effect were comedy dramas — a change of style heightened by the increasing use of straight actors such as Patrick Cargill in supporting roles rather than comic performers such as Fabrizi and Vyvyan. The shows' appeal remains undiminished by a quarter of a century's development of television, and indeed paved the way for the naturalistic situation comedies such as *Yes, Minister, Porridge, To the Manor Born* and *The Good Life* in which straight actors with comic ability were used to create convincing characters. Alan Simpson sums it up: 'We've been looking at the whole surviving output — some of them for the first time in twenty years — and you suddenly realize just how good he was, and how good Sid was. You didn't realize it at the time, you were too close to it — but when you look at them with hindsight you realize what a great performer the man was.'

PREVIOUS PAGES:
Hancock's Half-Hour. 'Underpaid!, or, Grandad's S.O.S.' (broadcast 2 January 1959). By the fourth TV series, of which this was the second programme, the team were well settled into the use of television. In this show, Hancock hears an S.O.S. on the radio asking him to contact his grandfather, Kitchener Hancock, who is ill, in Australia. Kitchener Hancock was a millionaire when last heard of, so Sid and Hancock assume that he wants to leave Hancock his fortune. But Hancock's assets total about £3 10s. (This is a rehearsal shot for the show, which perhaps explains the Father Christmas outfit — which is not part of the plot.)

LEFT:
'Underpaid!, or, Grandad's S.O.S.'
Sid had shown little interest in Hancock's grandfather —
until learning about the millionaire part of it. He insists
that, somehow or other, Hancock must get out to Australia
as quickly as possible. But how on earth are they going to
raise the fare?

ABOVE:
'Underpaid!, or, Grandad's S.O.S.'. Sid and Hancock
decide to raise money by busking, and hire musicians Johnny
Vyvyan (left) and Mario Fabrizi on a promise from Sid of 10
per cent of the gross and 3 per cent of anything over £5,000.
After three and a half hours of 'Friends and Neighbours' the
haul is 5s 6d.

LEFT:

'The Flight of the Red Shadow' (23 January 1959). Hancock and Sid have been with a touring company of The Desert Song — *and have decamped with the company's takings. However, Hancock's only clothing is his costume.*

ABOVE:

'The Flight of the Red Shadow'.

They set up business in Petticoat Lane, with Hancock telling fortunes — posing as a somewhat unlikely Indian. He is mistaken for a genuine Maharajah, and finds himself addressing a meeting . . . but the misunderstandings lead Hancock and Sid into prison — where they organize an inmates' performance of Rose Marie.

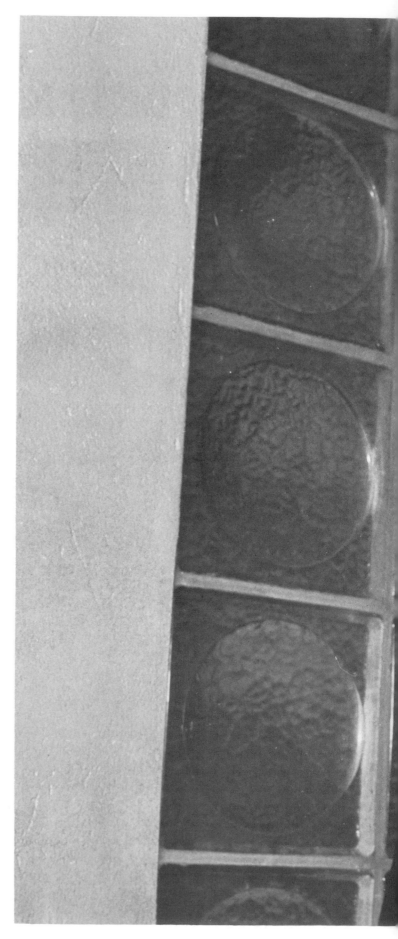

'Matrimony — Almost' (13 February 1959). Hancock is about to be married to the daughter of an apparently rich family. He is still puzzled: 'I can't understand it — why am I so desirable all of a sudden? I've been knocking about for 34 years and never a nibble. All of a sudden — wallop! This rich bird cottons on to me, and inside two weeks it's eyes down for a plateful of wedding cake!'

The reason is that Hancock met her at a pyjama party thrown by Sid in Hancock's house for the rich set. Because Hancock was wearing pyjamas (he was actually trying to get to sleep) she assumed that he was one of the group; and Sid told her that Hancock was very rich. However, her family is bankrupt, and she is really marrying Hancock for his supposed fortune. Of course it all goes wrong, and Hancock resolves: 'Once bitten twice shy — I'm not going to bed in pyjamas again'.

LEFT:
Not a Hancock's Half-Hour *fantasy sequence: on 9 February 1958 Hancock appeared in a television adaptation of Gogol's satirical play* The Government Inspector. *He played a good-for-nothing who is mistaken by the people of a small town for a visiting Inspector, and becomes the surprised recipient of their hospitality — and bribes. Although straight drama with no audience present was an unfamiliar field for Hancock he gave an excellent performance.*

ABOVE:
Hancock and Sid clown at rehearsals.

ABOVE:

Hancock's Half-Hour. *The fifth series began with 'The Economy Drive' (25 September 1959). Hancock and Sid return from holiday to find that everything has been left switched on — the television, the electric fire, even the washing machine ('All the water has evaporated, and what has happened to the shirts we shall never know!') — and that there are 150 pints of milk on the doorstep and two months' supply of newspapers blocking the hall. Determined to save money, Hancock decides to eat his lunch in a cheap self-service cafeteria — a new experience for him. He gets into total confusion about the method of choosing a meal,*

and argues with the staff and customers. In the picture, he has failed to get anything onto his tray by the time he reaches the cashier (Patricia Hayes), while Mario Fabrizi (behind him in the queue) looks on scornfully.

RIGHT:

'The Economy Drive'. Having finally managed to select and pay for a meal, Hancock sits down at a table with his lunch — but as he turns round to borrow a spoon from the table behind him one of the staff assumes he has finished and removes his tray.

'The Economy Drive'. Hancock's insistence on saving money by not using any electricity results in both of them falling down stairs in the dark. The resultant period in hospital costs them all the savings they had made, because Hancock had been saving money by not paying their National Insurance stamps — and upon returning home they find the doorstep piled high with milk bottles, the hall jammed with newspapers . . .

'The Two Murderers' (2 October 1959). Having checked carefully that Sid is out, Hancock is counting his savings: 'Enough there to get anything I want in the world — but I'm not going to 'cos I'd sooner have the money'. Some of the coins have a sentimental value: 'Hello — the three pennies that were thrown at me during the Royal Command Performance. Very embarrassing, that was — particularly when everybody saw where they came from.'

When Sid arrives Hancock hides the money in a hurry; Sid is suspicious of Hancock's behaviour: 'Have you had a bird in here?' 'That's a very unfair remark if I've ever heard one.'

Sid wants to borrow money from Hancock to start a fish-and-chip shop; Hancock sensibly refuses.

LEFT:
'The Two Murderers'. Sid has in fact now borrowed the money from a bank, but Hancock, seeing a book Sid was reading, Perfect Murders of the Twentieth Century, conceives the idea that Sid is out to murder him for his money. 'This is like Agatha Christie — it's like the Ten Little Indians — and I'm all ten of 'em!'

In the meantime Sid gets the same idea about Hancock, and with both of them in fear for their lives, neuroses reign supreme. In the end, the misunderstandings are resolved — but each of them brings a bodyguard to breakfast.

ABOVE:
Rehearsals; Hancock and Sid James.

FOLLOWING PAGE:
Breaks in rehearsals were usually spent playing snooker. Sid James coaches Hancock in a difficult shot.

TOP:

Face to Face. *On 7 February 1960 Hancock appeared in the series of half-hour 'in-depth' interviews by John Freeman. These were much more searching and harsh than would be normal today for someone in the entertainment world, and Freeman exposed Hancock's weaknesses and uncertainties ruthlessly. Hancock himself was satisfied with the result, and gave permission for the recording to be broadcast, but it is probable that the whole experience did him no good psychologically.*

BOTTOM:

The caption cards for Face to Face *used drawings of the interviewee each week by Feliks Topolski; here Hancock poses for the artist.*

'Twelve Angry Men' (16 October 1959). A skit on the famous film starring Henry Fonda. Everyone except Hancock thinks the defendant is guilty — including Sid; but Sid has discovered that jurors are paid 30s a day — more than he gets outside ('Let's keep this going as long as we can'). Hancock launches into a persuasive speech: 'Does Magna Carta mean nothing to you? Did she die in vain? — the brave Hungarian peasant girl who forced King John to sign the pledge at Runnymede and close the boozers at half-past ten!'

After some hours the final juror relents just to shut Hancock up: 'Let him loose so that he can rob other people's shops, other people's houses, your house maybe — I don't mind!' Hancock thinks for a moment: 'I've been thinking what he said, about letting him loose to rob people's shops and other people's houses — I couldn't have that on me conscience — I'll have to change me mind: guilty!'

Hancock and Sid James relax during studio rehearsals. The stuffed eagle was a regular part of the dowdy set of 23 Railway Cuttings.

December 1959. Simpson, Hancock and Galton look pleased with themselves, and so they might — the Guild of TV Producers and Directors had just voted Hancock 'Best Light Entertainment Personality' of the year, and Galton and Simpson 'Best Scriptwriters'.

Hancock's Half-Hour. *The sixth series began on 4 March 1960 with 'The Cold'. Hancock is ill; Sid is unsympathetic. Hancock: 'All me red corpuscles are hiding away in corners frightened to come out, and I don't blame 'em! I don't blame 'em with the sort of germs I get — I get big ones with the hairy legs and pointed teeth like you see in the kitchen sink adverts.'*

FOLLOWING PAGES — LEFT:
'The Cold'. Sid can't see what Hancock is making such a fuss about. Hancock: 'It's all right for you, you never get anything wrong with you! Six colds I've had this year, and you haven't had a thing — not a sniffle! It's not fair — I object — why couldn't we have had three each?'

TOP RIGHT:
'The Cold'. Despairing of his patent medicines, Hancock calls in Mrs Cravatte (Patricia Hayes) and her health cures. She sticks a twig in his mouth: 'It's a freshly cut twig from an 'orse chestnut tree — it's one what 'asn't borne any conkers for the past three seasons. If your blood's got the fever the sap will rise . . . watch that leaf — if that withers and dies, you'll follow it within the week.' She makes strange movements in front of him which she describes as 'drawing out' his cold; Hancock is suspicious: 'I'm not having any cockerels strangled over me bedclothes — or any live toads sitting in a semicircle, I'm not having any of that!' When he coughs, she produces an aerosol spray — 'I don't want to catch your cold, do I?'

BOTTOM RIGHT:
'The Cold'. After getting no help from a doctor (who recommends him to try Mrs Cravatte) Hancock takes up a suggestion from Sid that the best cure is exercise. After a tough regime of runs and sparring at the local gym, Hancock has no cold, but he's sprained his wrist, he can't bend his leg or his neck, and his feet are covered in blisters. He decides he'd rather have a cold. Sid sneezes. Hancock: 'That's my cold and I want it back!' With the first developing sign of a snuffle he happily settles back to his medicines.

'The Missing Page' (11 March 1960). Within seconds of entering the local library Hancock becomes involved in a shushing match with everyone else. He is then joined by Sid, whose reactions to being shushed are violent. Hancock: 'Sid, please, no punch-ups on municipal property'. Shushed again when trying to describe the plot of a thriller, Hancock launches into a complicated (and beautifully executed) piece of mime in which he manages to be all the characters in the book.

'The Missing Page'. Hancock's mime is interrupted by the librarian (Hugh Lloyd); 'What do you think you're doing? This is a library, not the Royal Academy of Dramatic Art!' Sid takes exception to all this and has to be restrained again. Hancock: 'Sid, come away, don't show me up — you're always starting something! I do apologize, it's not his fault, he can't help it — he can't stand rules and regulations, it's the gypsy in him.'

'The Missing Page'. Hancock is excited by the thriller he has
brought from the library: 'This is red hot, this is, mate — I'd
hate to think of a book like this getting into the wrong hands.
As soon as I've finished this I shall recommend they ban it.'
His excitement turns to frustration when he discovers that
the last page is missing, and the rest of the show is concerned
with his attempts to find another copy to find out how the
story ended.

   Only after a lot of research does he realize that the author
died before completing it, and the book had been published
without the ending.

Hancock and Sid rehearse — possibly for 'The Missing Page' — without cameras, costume or even props, in what seems to be a gymnasium.

'The Emigrant' (18 March 1960). Hancock, wanting to emigrate, has picked his destination with a pin on the map: the first choice was Baffin Land, but a more satisfactory one was Australia. Arriving at Australia House with his belongings he discusses immigration with the clerk. He has to admit to his age ('thirtyish') and his criminal record ('Two parking offences, one loitering, and one drunk in charge of a petrol-driven lawnmower'). Rejected for Australia, he tries Canada House; the clerk (Gordon Sterne, in the picture) asks 'Is there any insanity in your family?' Hancock: 'Do you mind? How dare you drag my uncle into this?'

'The Emigrant'. Rejected by Australia, Canada, India,
South Africa, New Zealand, the Christmas Islands and even
Baffin Land, Hancock is in despair ('As for the Friendly
Islands, how they got their name I do not know!'). Sid, who
has had some experience in getting people in or out of various
countries, is persuaded to help, and for £150 Hancock is
booked onto a ship. Arriving blindfolded, for 'security
reasons', he is told he is to go on a luxury liner. 'Is it the
Queen Mary?' Sid: 'Well . . . no, it's not the Queen Mary —
same sort of thing, not quite so big.'

ABOVE:

'The Emigrant'. The 'luxury liner' is, needless to say, a thoroughly disreputable tramp steamer with a drunken captain and a crew of toughs. Sid tells them to put Hancock off at the first bit of coastline they come to and makes a quick getaway. The crew grab Hancock's luggage and start dividing it up among themselves; and when Hancock takes his blindfold off he discovers he is sharing his 'cabin' with a cow.

RIGHT:

'The Emigrant'. In the last scene, Hancock is found at his final destination — Baffin Land. He is trying to catch fish through a hole in the ice. 'Three weeks I've been up here — not a nibble.' He is offered advice by an Eskimo. Hancock: 'Well, why didn't you tell me before, you fur-clad fool! (Pointing behind him) He's just told me the sea starts here! He saw me digging that hole! (Shouting through the hole) Come out, come on! — get hold of this hook — I know you're down there! Come on out . . . all right, stay there, suit yourself . . .'

'The Reunion Party' (25 March 1960). Hancock has arranged a reunion of his wartime army mates, whom he has not seen for fifteen years. At the off-licence he places an order for enough alcohol to stock a pub: 'That's just to clear the dust out of their throats . . . the Third East Cheam Light Horse — three of the heaviest drinkers who ever set foot inside a pair of army boots . . . There'll be some high jinks down the Cuttings tomorrow night — you won't be able to hear the trains going by.'

TOP LEFT:
'The Reunion Party'. All Hancock's old army friends have changed beyond recognition. Ginger Johnson (Clive Dunn) was once the life and soul of the party — now he is bald and very subdued, and, to make matters more depressing, mistakes Hancock for one of the others. (This picture is a frame enlargement from the telerecording.)

BOTTOM LEFT:
'Sid in Love' (1 April 1960). Sitting in the fish-and-chip shop after a visit to the cinema, Hancock realizes that Sid is unhappy: 'Did the film upset you?' . . . Was it the Tweetie Pie when the cat had all his teeth knocked out?'. Sid eventually admits to being in love with a clippie on the 93 bus: 'She goes past every morning just as I'm getting me socks in off the windowsill — I smile at her, and I wave, and she doesn't take a blind bit of notice'. Hancock offers to chat her up on Sid's behalf: 'By the time I've finished with her she'll think she's going to marry Cary Grant'.

ABOVE:
'Sid in Love'. Hancock takes Sid onto the bus to meet his clippie (Joan Heal) and starts to chat her up on Sid's behalf: 'Good Heavens! Don't move! This is remarkable, I wouldn't have believed it . . . You're Shirley Eaton, aren't you?' The clippie comments that it's a bit early in the evening for the drunks. Hancock: 'Do you mean to say you're not Shirley Eaton?' The clippie: 'Well of course I'm not . . . I suppose we do do our hair a bit similar.' Hancock makes a plea on behalf of Sid — 'How would you like to step out with Cary Grant here?' 'Are you kidding? I'd want a Government grant to go out with him.'

Hancock's approaches eventually get them thrown off the bus — and Hancock into deep trouble with the bus-driver, who is also the clippie's husband.

Hancock's last series for BBC Television, under the title
Hancock, *began on 26 May 1961 with 'The Bedsitter', a*
remarkable solo performance. Deciding to improve his mind,
Hancock tries to read Bertrand Russell's Human
Knowledge, its limits and scope. *Within a few seconds of*
starting the introduction he has to refer to the dictionary:
'Well if that's what they mean, why don't they say so? . . .
Oh, I don't know what he's talking about — "The Limit and
Scope of Human Knowledge" — well, we've soon found out
my limit, haven't we!'

THE
UNIVERSAL
ENGLISH
DICTIONARY

Edited by
HENRY CECIL WYLD
Late Merton Professor of English Language and Literature
in the University of Oxford

With an Appendix by
ERIC PARTRIDGE

'As a single-volume dictionary, in a class by itself.'
The Times Literary Supplement

'Can be recommended without any qualification
whatever.'
The Daily Telegraph

ROUTLEDGE &
KEGAN PAUL

'The Bedsitter'. Hancock continues the struggle with Bertrand Russell. 'I should know, it's in English — I should know what he's talking about — he's a human being, the same as me, using English words available to us all — now, concentrate. . . . No, it's him — it's him that's at fault, he's a rotten writer. A good writer should be able to put down his thoughts clearly in the simplest terms understandable to everybody — it's him! He's a bad writer — I'm not going to waste my time reading him.'

LEFT:
'The Bedsitter'. Hancock has fixed up a date, and prepares himself: 'Ah, you can't beat the cold steel and the badger! All this electrical rubbish, little wheels spinning around all over the place — that's for callow youths and peach fluff, not for a man's beard! "Razor blades, for men!"' A moustache of shaving-soap prompts him into a Harold Macmillan impersonation — 'You've never had it so good — the winds of change . . .'.

Needless to say, the date rings up to cry off, leaving Hancock to amuse himself for the evening: 'We'll have one more go at Bert [Russell] I think, see how we get on with him . . . no, I'll read it tomorrow'.

FOLLOWING PAGES:
'The Bowmans' (2 June 1961). Hancock is the Walter Gabriel-type character in a radio soap opera similar to The Archers. Also with him in the picture are Peter Glaze (left) as the dog (and all the other farmyard animals), Brian Oulton as 'Dan Bowman' and Constance Chapman as 'Gladys Bowman'. Hancock's frequent rural ad-libs irritate the other actors and cause loud canine protests from Peter Glaze in an attempt to get Hancock back on the script. Hancock: 'I'm warning you — one more yelp from you and you get this down your throat!'

'The Bowmans'. Hancock is upset to be told by the producer that his character is to be killed off in the next episode. The character is falling off in popularity. Hancock: 'It's the scriptwriters — they're making me far too unsympathetic — last week I kicked the dog three times'. The producer: 'Well that was not in the script'. Hancock: 'Well no, but he asked for it, shoving in yelps . . .'.

The producer also complains about Hancock's variable accent: 'Last week I could swear we had a bit of Robert Newton in there'. Hancock is furious at the criticism: 'You come in here — an ex-sound-mixer for Sports Report — and talk to me about acting?'

In the end the character is killed off — but has to be reinstated (in the form of a twin brother) by public demand, and Hancock uses the opportunity to dominate the entire show by having the rest of the cast killed off.

'The Radio Ham' (9 June 1961). Hancock has entered the fascinating world of amateur radio. His first contact of the evening is with Tokyo: 'Yoki! — how are you? . . . no, no, how — are — you . . . how are you ? . . . This Rondon GLK, how getting are you?' He enquires about the weather in Japan: 'I cannot understand . . . say it slowly . . . put it another way . . . in English. It — is — are — raining — not . . . oh, good . . . it is are raining not here, also.'

'The Radio Ham'. Hancock has made contact with a mayday call — a motor-yacht in distress (the voice of Andrew Faulds). He wastes time looking for a pencil to take down the yacht's position, and then loses contact at the crucial moment. When he re-establishes contact the mayday call is very annoyed with him: 'Pull yourself together, for heaven's sake!' Hancock: 'Now look here, my good man, don't you take that tone of voice with me — I'm doing my best, it's not my fault you've got a hole in your boat! You should learn how to steer it properly in the first place.'

Then his attempts to take down the position are interrupted by the neighbours complaining about the noise, and the sudden failure of his valves. When he finally gets operational again he hears that the yachtsman's call has been picked up by the Japanese radio ham, and he has been rescued. Disgusted, Hancock returns to his radio — only to pick up another distress call: 'If I were you I should get on to somebody else — it'll be much quicker in the long run.'

'The Lift' (16 June 1961). Hancock has insisted on being the ninth person in a Television Centre lift which is supposed to carry only eight — and the lift has stuck between floors. Trapped with him are (left to right in the picture) the lift operator (Hugh Lloyd), Jack Watling, Diana King, John Le Mesurier (behind her), Colin Gordon, Noel Howlett, José Reed and Charles Lloyd Pack. The lift operator instructs them to stand with their knees bent to absorb any sudden movements of the lift while he presses the emergency button — but nothing happens.

RIGHT:
'The Lift'. The Air Marshall (John Le Mesurier) suggests
they all shout for help. Hancock: 'Good idea. Thank heavens
for the military mind in an emergency — Cranwell has
triumphed again.' But their shouts are unheard, and they
have to settle down for a long night in the lift, not made any
easier by Hancock's attempts to keep their morale up by
relating his supposed wartime experiences in a submarine.

FOLLOWING PAGE:
'The Lift'. Hancock entertains the others with charades.
This is the first syllable of I Was A Teenage Werewolf; but
as the TV producer (Jack Watling) guesses the answer every
time — even before Hancock has finished — he soon loses
interest and the others settle down thankfully to get some
sleep.

'The Lift'. In the morning they are rescued, but Hancock
unwisely goes back into the lift to look for his season ticket,
and finds himself trapped once again, this time with only the
lift operator. Happily they settle down to charades.
Hancock: 'It's much better this, the two of us, isn't it . . . you
know, I didn't like you at the beginning — it's funny, I was
quite wrong about you.

ABOVE.
'The Blood Donor' (23 June 1961). Hancock's most lastingly famous show. He arrives at the clinic having seen an advertisement encouraging him to give blood: 'I've been thinking about this for a long time — something for the benefit of the country as a whole — what should it be, I thought? Become a blood donor or join the Young Conservatives? Anyway, as I'm not looking for a wife and I can't play table-tennis, here I am.'

RIGHT.
'The Blood Donor'. Hancock waits nervously to see the doctor. 'Do you get a badge for doing this? . . . We should have something for people to pick us out by . . . You know, nothing grand, a little enamel thing, a motto, that's all — nothing pretentious — something like "He Gave It for Others So That Others May Live". We are do-gooders, we should get something for it.'

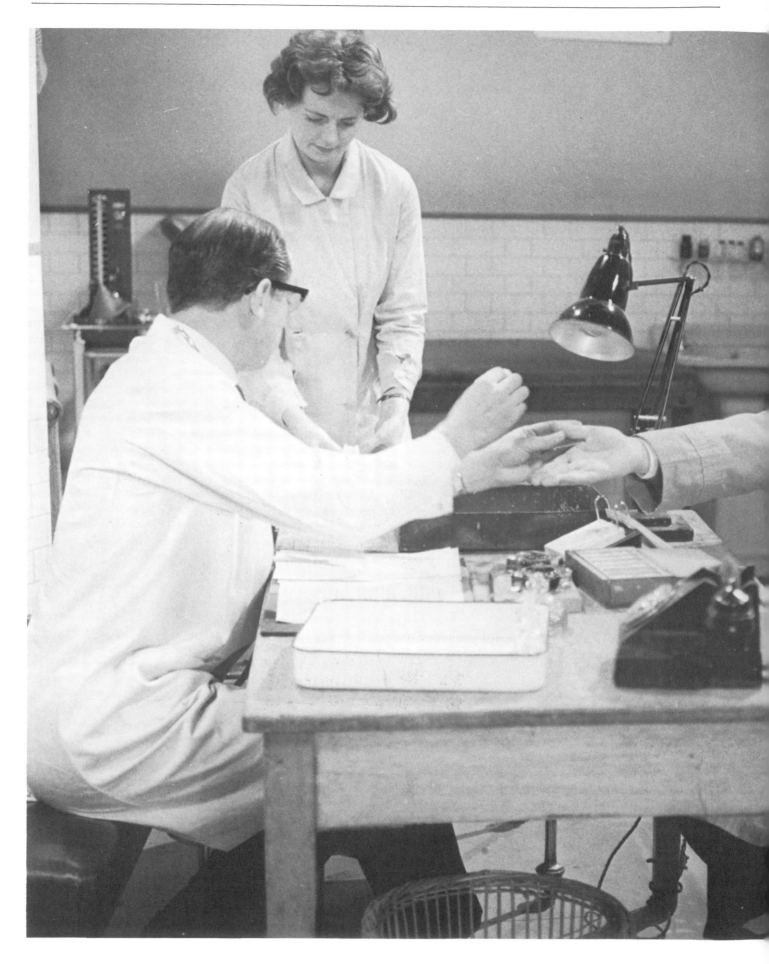

'The Blood Donor'. The doctor (Patrick Cargill) and the nurse (Anne Marryott) take a smear from Hancock's thumb; Hancock thinks that that is all there is to it. 'It may be just a smear to you, mate, but it's life and death to some poor wretch!' He is told that a normal donation is a pint. 'A pint? Have you gone raving mad? I don't mind giving a reasonable amount, but a pint — that's very nearly an armful! I'm sorry, I'm not walking around with an empty arm for anybody.'

He is persuaded into giving the pint, on the grounds that he has a very rare blood group; he steels himself — and passes out as the first drop flows.

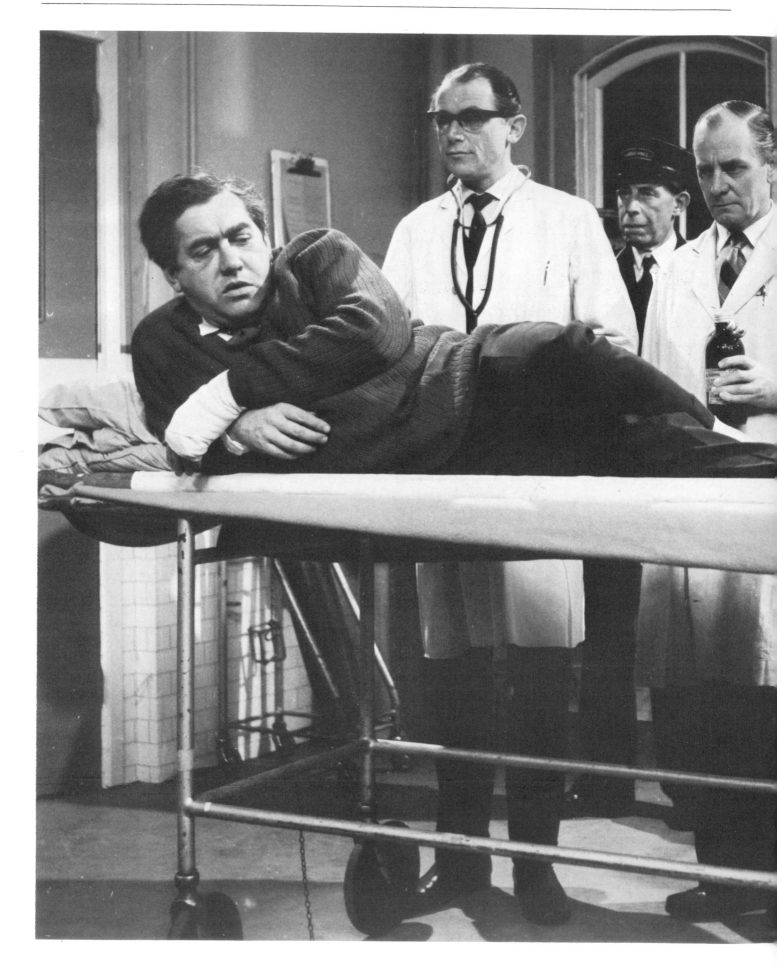

'The Blood Donor'. The next day, Hancock cuts himself severely on a bread-knife and is taken to hospital, where the doctors (Patrick Cargill and James Ottoway) and a nurse (Jean Marlow) prepare to give him a transfusion of the only blood they have in his group. The doctor: 'He only gave it yesterday! Waste of time, wasn't it!' Hancock: 'Well, I'd have been in a right state if I hadn't — there's nothing else here for me! At least I know it's going to the right sort of person. These blood banks are just like ordinary banks, really — put it in when you're flush, draw it out when you need it . . .'

In his last BBC show, 'The Succession — Son and Heir' (30 June 1961), Hancock has decided that it is time he got married and produced an heir. Narrowing the field to three girls, he proposes first to Olive Hobbs, who wants to call their son Elvis, so Hancock withdraws his application. The second is the intellectual Veronica Stillwell (June Whitfield, in the picture) who accepts the idea of the furtherance of the race, but regards marriage as an outmoded institution and will enter only into a free liaison. Hancock: 'A liaison? What are you suggesting? My mother would never have that. I mean, living up here on me own in London is bad enough!'

She storms out, calling him a weak-minded traditionalist wallowing in a morass of respectability. Hancock: 'Dear, oh, dear — the people you meet — I never thought I'd hear a vicar's daughter talk like that!'

'The Succession — Son and Heir'. Hancock's last attempt — the Honourable Pamela Ffortescue-Ffrench — is going little better, when the other two girls burst in. (Gwenda Ewan, on the left, as Pamela, June Whitfield as Veronica, and Myrtle Reed as Olive.) Olive promises not to call their son Elvis and to go to night school; Veronica has decided that the furtherance of the race is more important and agrees to marriage. A row breaks out between the girls; Hancock tries to intervene and is told to keep out of it. Packing his suitcase, he leaves: 'So exits the last of the Hancocks. Good luck!'

INDEPENDENT TELEVISION

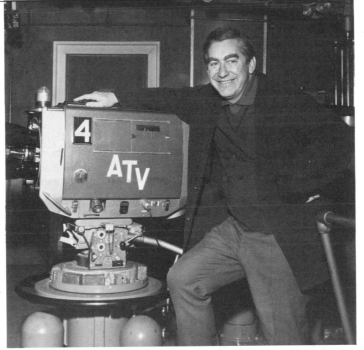

Hancock's very first television series was made for one of the ITV companies, Associated-Rediffusion, and arose out of his contractual obligations to Jack Hylton (for whom he had been appearing in *The Talk of the Town* at the Adelphi Theatre). Under the title *The Tony Hancock Show* this series of six programmes began on 27 April 1956; he then made his first BBC TV series, and then a second series, also of six programmes, for Hylton. After this he made no more appearances on ITV, being under an exclusive BBC contract, until 1963.

At the time when the first Hylton series was made, ITV was still very new — transmission had begun only the previous September — and the shows suffered from some technical rough edges. However, some of the material was effectively written for the Hancock character as it stood at that time. The format of the show was a series of sketches, in which Hancock appeared with supporting artists such as June Whitfield, Clive Dunn, Dick Emery and John Vere. Although not up to the standard of the Galton and Simpson shows which were to follow, there are some good moments — in particular a sudden launch by Hancock into his Punch-and-Judy impression, crossing his arms, holding a gavel as Mr Punch's stick, and flopping about muttering 'That's the way to do it'.

The scripts were written by Eric Sykes, who remembers: 'At that time I was struggling to find something to hang my hat on, and so they were variable — one or two of the ideas were Tony's himself, and I wrote them up, so we were trying to get together on a way of working. Only Tony was such a perfectionist that he had to learn every word exactly; as a result, come the day before the programme I was not allowed to change a word.'

No recordings survive of the second Hylton series, for which Galton and Simpson contributed some material anonymously, but the basic format was the same, consisting of sketches with a few interspersed musical numbers. At the end of each of the first series programmes a demonstration of straight dancing — in a different style each week — was worked into the sketch, which Hancock and Whitfield would then parody.

After the last BBC TV series ended in 1961 Hancock made the film *The Punch and Judy Man* (dealt with in the next section), and then came to another ITV company, ATV, to make a series of thirteen programmes. He acted as his own executive producer — which placed additional demands upon him which were no help to his performances. The director was Alan Tarrant, who had been doing production, but was happy to take what was in effect a step down to direction in order to work with Hancock, whom he greatly admired.

The initial handful of scripts were written by Godfrey Harrison, a skilled writer of long experience, who wrote *A Life of Bliss* for radio. Harrison wrote some good material for Hancock, but tended to overwrite and also to turn scripts in late. After six programmes he was replaced by Terry Nation — not yet famous as the creator of the Daleks in *Doctor Who* — and then, in an increasing atmosphere of worry, by Richard Harris and Dennis Spooner. Their scripts were not of a very high standard, but it would not be fair to judge them on these programmes because they were writing under pressure for a performer with whom they were not familiar, and inevitably they could not hope to match their work to Hancock's character.

One of the difficulties that many of the shows suffered from was that Hancock's pomposity and aggressive behaviour were no longer balanced by his more likeable characteristics, as Galton and Simpson point out. Ray Galton: 'You had to have a *reason* for his being pompous and nasty, and we always provided that as a matter of course. But that was thrown away and Tony was unnecessarily nasty; you can't be nasty without a reason and be funny.' Alan Simpson: 'To be nasty after you've been rejected is reasonable; to be nasty *before* you've been rejected is gratuitous.' Galton: 'It's an unbelievably basic mistake that everybody made, including Tony'.

However, provided that direct comparisons with the best of the BBC work are avoided, several of the shows in the ATV series are well worth watching. They had very high production standards, and Hancock was surrounded by straight actors rather than comics — and actors of a high calibre, including Martita Hunt, Allan Cuthbertson, Denholm Elliott, Geoffrey Keen, James Villiers and Derek Nimmo. Some of the scripts are well thought out and effectively written. In 'Shooting Star' (17 January 1963), Hancock gets involved with a team making a documentary film, and his complete failure to cope with the simplest instructions once the cameras are turning is extremely funny. In 'The Politician' (7 March 1963) he strikes up an acquaintance with a street-corner speaker (John Le Mesurier). He is encouraged to heckle the speaker as a means of drawing a crowd; but the speaker is well able to cope with Hancock's interruptions and Hancock finds himself under attack from a woman in the crowd for insulting an older man: 'You ought to be horsewhipped!' Hancock: 'Well that dates *you*, for a start'. The next day Hancock, fancying himself as a public speaker, attempts to get an uninterested elderly passer-by to heckle him in the same manner; but although Hancock tries to use the same ripostes that the original speaker had used on him, the passer-by will not co-operate, and Hancock finds himself under attack from the same woman, once again for insulting an older man.

Then the original speaker arrives, and helps Hancock to get started; but a crowd of roughs attempts to pick a fight. Hancock, unwilling to admit cowardice ('I could sort you out with one hand tied behind me back') agrees to a fight, but only once the meeting is over — and keeps it going until a policeman comes by, two hours or so later. The next day the original speaker is unable to persuade Hancock to have another go — Hancock has lost his voice.

'The Politician' was written by Terry Nation, who also wrote 'The Assistant', one of the most successful shows, in which Hancock, unable to pay his account at a department store, is taken on as an assistant with the promise that his debt will be cancelled if he can work for a week without being rude to the customers. In point of fact we never find out whether he wins his wager — a weakness in the overall construction of the plot, since the show has no real resolution — but there are some good scenes in various of the shop's departments as Hancock attempts to remain polite while faced with intractable customers, irritating children, and a ridiculous 'Uncle Bunny' costume he is forced to wear.

Alan Tarrant found working with Hancock a fascinating, if increasingly fraught, experience: 'He was a very interesting chap when he was relaxing. I remember him talking about philosophy, and he gave a sort of Cockney version of various philosophies, which was hilariously funny. And he was like the character he played in a strange sort of way; he was a nervous man — he started off in the forces, of course, and he told me that once when he was having a big dinner with Harry Secombe after a show he said to Harry, "You know — we should be at the NAAFI now" — he couldn't get over the fact that he had got so far so fast. He couldn't believe it.'

Halfway through the series Hancock suddenly turned up with a very short haircut, which was far from flattering to him, and this, plus the increasing difficulties with production, make his performances in the later shows in the series look rather worrying. Harris and Spooner did the best they could with the scripts, but they placed too much reliance on Hancock's fantasy life; and in 'The Early Call' (14 February 1963) they required Hancock to carry most of the show on his own, as he had previously done in 'The Bedsitter'. It was a miscalculation, because neither their script nor Hancock's performance were up to such a demanding task.

Their script for 'The Escort' (28 March 1963) is rather better, and contains some good ideas. Hancock has never come across the idea of professional (male) escorts until one is pointed out to him. It is suggested that he should try for a job as one: 'What, me, soil me hands with money for doing what I've been doing all me natural?'. However, he applies to the agency, representing himself as an ex-Guardsman with scars from a fencing duel at Heidelberg University who speaks six languages 'fluidly'. The agency owner, attempting to assess Hancock's knowledge of manners, asks how he would address an Archbishop. Hancock: 'Your brochure never said anything about going out with Archbishops'. He is told: 'If we ever have a fencing-mistress who speaks six languages "fluidly" and is partial to small guardsmen, we'll call you. Until then, get out.'

In the end the agency, in order to get rid of him, send him out with a boisterous rough-tongued rich Australian woman. They go out for a meal — at a workmen's cafe in Stepney, where even Hancock's limited table manners are out of place; he asks an Irish navvy to pass the condiments: 'I'd be delighted to — if I knew what they was'. The navvy eventually passes over the salt and pepper — and the HP sauce, the salad cream, the vinegar and several other things. Hancock: 'I want to eat it, not suffocate it'. Then the Irishman picks up Hancock's companion and they go off, leaving Hancock. In the final scene Hancock has discovered that men who model suits get their clothes free, and is considering a new career ...

In 1965 Hancock made a series of very funny TV commercials for the Egg Marketing Board, with Patricia Hayes as his landlady, Mrs Cravatte; and then in 1966 and 1967 made his last two British TV series, both for ABC-TV. The first, *The Blackpool Show*, was recorded in the summer of 1966 in the ABC Theatre, Blackpool, and was a series of hour-long variety shows, with Hancock acting (somewhat uncertainly) as compère and performing sketches solo and with John Junkin. The results were variable, though the best of Hancock's sketches were effective enough. Junkin made a good stooge — named 'Evelyn', which gave Hancock plenty of opportunities for suitable facial reaction — and some of Hancock's old routines, such as 'The Crooner' were re-worked by the writers, John Muir and Eric Geen. (Junkin: 'Sinatra does two hours out there with just a hat.' Hancock: 'Well, get off and get me a hat. Sinatra — who's he?')

The final series, *Hancock's*, was transmitted in June and July 1967. With Muir and Geen again the writers, the premise was that Hancock was the owner — and the waiter, bartender and half the cabaret — in a nightclub. They wrote a number of sketches to fit into the situation, and the show was bolstered up by the inclusion of guest acts such as Vikki Carr and Marian Montgomery, supposedly performing in Hancock's club. There were some good lines in the sketches: June Whitfield: 'You look rather foolish dressed like that — a man of your build.' Hancock: 'I am not a man of my build'. However by this time Hancock's personal difficulties had reached a point when he was unable to give a performance with anything like his old abilities, and the series was inevitably a failure.

Apart from a couple of interviews on chat shows, he made no more appearances on British television. He went to Australia in 1968 to make a colour TV series, but completed only three episodes — which have never been shown in Britain, and which do not make enjoyable viewing. However, the best of the 1963 ATV series — about the first half — still stands up quite well, and it is sad that he was unable to develop the ideas which were beginning to take shape in them.

The 1963 ATV shows were transmitted in a different order from that in which they were recorded. The first to go out was 'The Assistant' (broadcast 3 January 1963). Hancock, not realizing the glass is missing from a shop window, tries to lean against it and gets tangled up with an undressed dummy, much to his embarrassment.

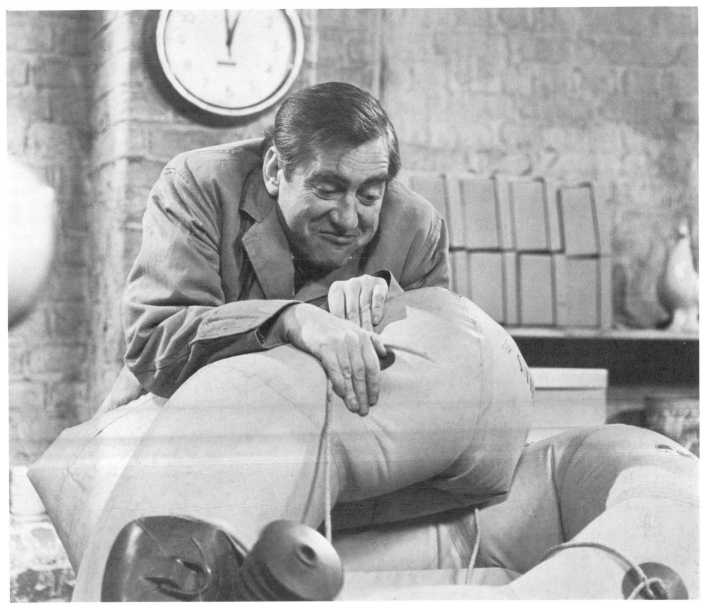

'The Assistant'. Hancock is taken on as an assistant with the promise that his outstanding account will be cancelled if he can work for a week without being rude to customers. He starts in the packing department, attempting to pack an inflatable dinghy which has just inflated itself — a problem he solves by stabbing it with the scissors.

'The Assistant'. Hancock is promoted to the children's department as 'Uncle Bunny'. The manager (Patrick Cargill) instructs him in his duties.

'The Assistant'. Hancock immediately gets into an argument with a little girl (Adrienne Poster, who later changed her stage name to Adrienne Posta).

He involves an elderly lady customer in a game of toy football, leaving her too exhausted to buy anything; and we never discover whether he succeeds in completing his week without being rude to anyone.

'The Man on the Corner' (31 January 1963). Each show started with Hancock standing on a street corner, getting involved in something which would then lead to the rest of the plot. Here the headline about the smashing of a spy ring convinces him that he has just seen a spy.

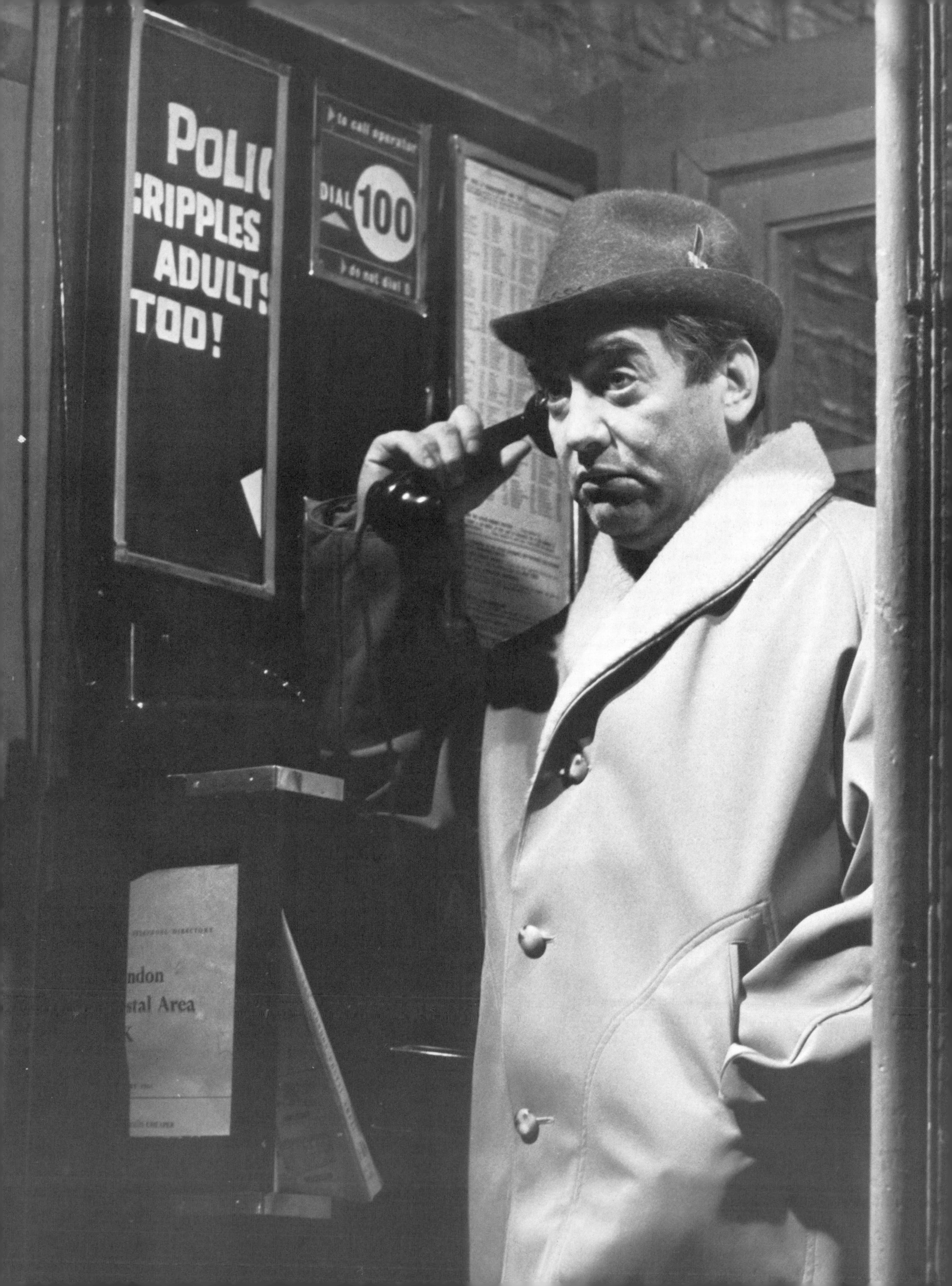
POLIC
CRIPPLES
ADULTS
TOO!
DIAL
100

LEFT:

'The Man on the Corner'. Hancock takes his suspicions to MI5, who 'enrol' him in the hope of keeping him quiet, a forlorn hope since Hancock sees spies in every corner.

ABOVE:

'The Memory Test' (7 February 1963). Hancock is asked to take part in a 'This is Your Life'-type programme about his old Wing-Commander; but Hancock cannot remember the man, and no amount of looking in reference books and old diaries seems to help.

'The Memory Test'. Hancock in the TV studio, with the presenter (Shaw Taylor, standing) and the Wing-Commander (Edward Chapman) whom he still cannot remember.

'The Early Call' (14 February 1963). Hancock is anxious to
wake up early but he does not trust his alarm clock. He books
an alarm call but then worries whether the telephone works.

'The Early Call'. The writers built up Hancock's fantasy life — picked up perhaps from his flights of fancy in earlier Galton and Simpson shows like 'The Bedsitter' — but had less success in integrating them into the plot.

'The Politician' (7 March 1963). Hancock has a go at public speaking, with the help of a little planned heckling from his friend (John Le Mesurier).

'The Reporter' (14 March 1963). Hancock becomes a
reporter on a local paper, and is sent to cover a smart society
wedding. His lack of tact soon causes havoc; here he talks to
the bride (Clare Owen).

ABOVE:
'The Reporter'. Hancock insults a wedding guest (Pauline Winter).

RIGHT:
'The Escort' (28 March 1963). Dressed up to the nines, Hancock waits for his first date as a professional escort — a rich but boisterous Australian the agency have chosen in order to get rid of him.

'The Escort'. The Australian (Maggie Fitzgibbon) and the owner of the workmen's cafe she has chosen (Arthur Lovegrove) wait for Hancock to make a selection from the menu.

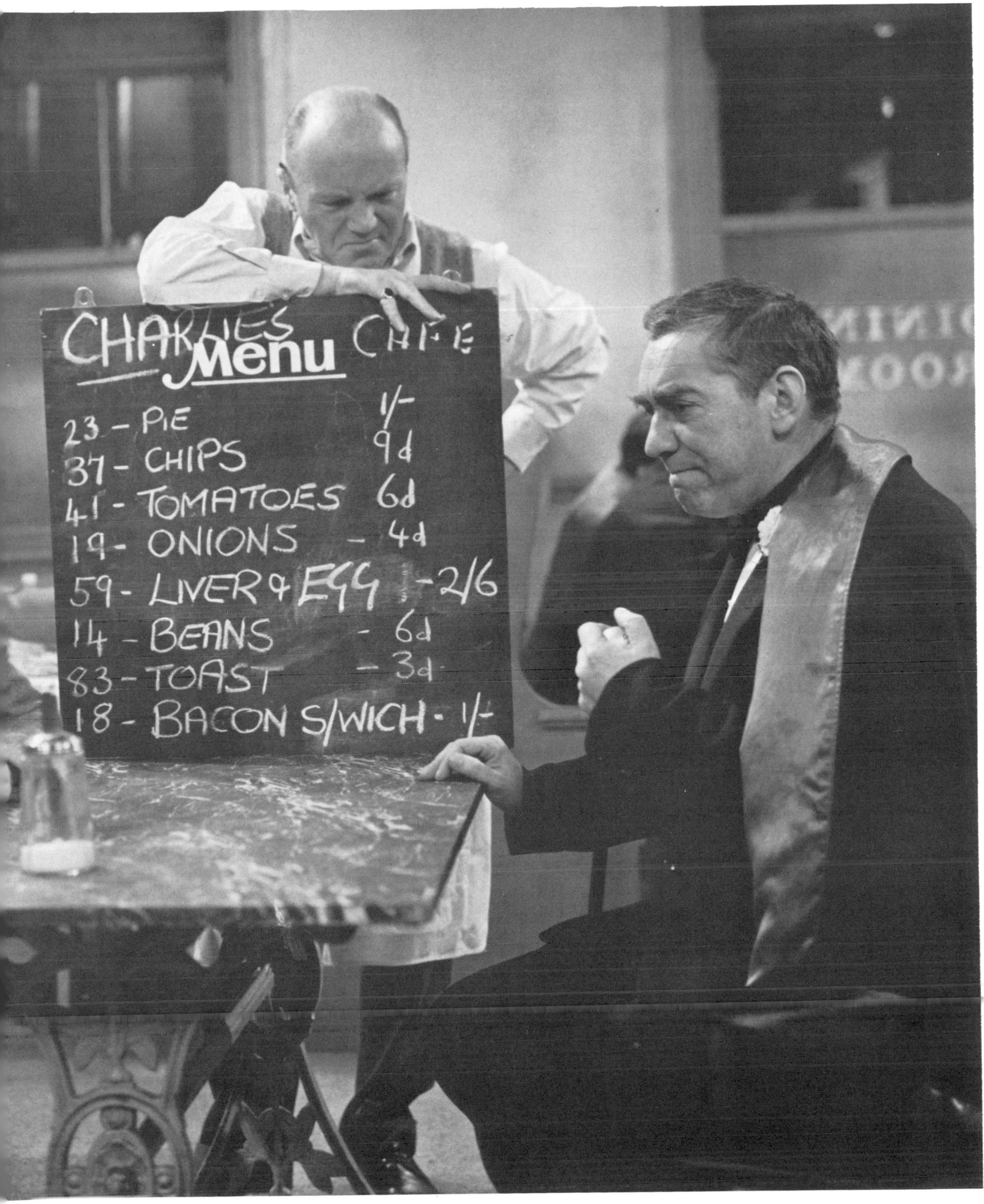

CHARLIES CAFE

Menu

23	PIE		1/-
37	CHIPS		9d
41	TOMATOES		6d
19	ONIONS	-	4d
59	LIVER & EGG	-	2/6
14	BEANS	-	6d
83	TOAST	-	3d
18	BACON S/WICH	-	1/-

LEFT:
On 12 December 1965 Hancock married Freddie Ross, who had been working as his publicist for some time. He managed to be late for the ceremony at Marylebone Register Office ('traffic problems' he explained) but it looks from this photograph, taken just after the ceremony, as if she has forgiven him.

FOLLOWING PAGES — LEFT:
The 1967 ABC-TV series Hancock's *starred Hancock as the owner of a nightclub. Each week he appeared in a different costume in an attempt to entertain the guests; here he plays a mean maraca.*

ABOVE:
In the summer of 1966 Hancock compered ABC-TV's variety series The Blackpool Show, *recorded in the ABC Theatre, Blackpool. Here he converses with 'Evelyn' — John Junkin — his stooge in some of the sketches.*

RIGHT:
Hancock's : *Hancock with a member of his staff, June Whitfield, who appeared as a waitress in all the shows.*

Hancock's *(30 June 1967). Hancock as a gypsy fiddler upsetting the digestions of customers Damaris Hayman and Frank Crawshaw.*

Hancock's: *Pop singer Hancock finds himself being questioned by the police.*

Hancock came to see cinema films as the medium which would give him the chance he wanted to become internationally recognized, although circumstances prevented him from making more than a few appearances. Ironically, his particular instinctive abilities were less suited to films than to television; despite the strains of TV, he could at least turn in a more or less continuous performance in the presence of an audience — whose reactions were vital to his judgement of timing — and see the result fairly shortly afterwards. In films he had to give his performance out of order, in small chunks, not seeing the final result for months after shooting had finished — a technique which demands the skills of a more calculating performer. However, his two starring roles are effective and well worth seeing.

His first film appearance was in the 1954 *Orders Are Orders*, a very poor comedy based on a 1932 play, set on an Army base which is invaded by a film company. Hancock's few scenes are the most effective in the film; he plays the bandmaster, and is seen rehearsing his band — including, in a brief appearance, Eric Sykes — in the pompous style associated with his *Educating Archie* character, for this was before the radio character was fully developed. Sydney James appeared in the unlikely guise of an American film producer, and the cast included Bill Fraser and Peter Sellers; but even so the film was a deserved failure.

Hancock made no more films until *The Rebel*, made in 1960 as the first under a new contract with Associated-British Films. Galton and Simpson wrote the screenplay, making good use of their experience with the character, and Hancock gave a sustained performance which was highly successful; indeed the film had a greater success than any other first starring feature for a British comedian, at any rate in the postwar period.

Hancock is first seen as a regimented clerk in an accounting office, who rebels by drawing faces in the ledger and hanging his umbrella the other way round from everyone else's. Rushing home, he returns enthusiastically to a huge and very ugly figure he is sculpting in his rooms — much to the disgust of his landlady, Mrs Cravatte (played this time by Irene Handl). She is not impressed by his statue — Hancock: 'That is women as I see them.' — 'Oh, you poor man!' — or by a painting showing beetroot-coloured ducks. 'Well, they fly at a fair lick, those ducks — they're up, out of the water, and away — you just have to whack on whatever you've got on to the brush at the time!'

Determined to escape his constrained life, he goes to Paris, where he makes friends with Paul, an English painter (Paul Massie). His self-confidence, rather than his artistic abilities, soon makes him the centre of the attentions of the artistic crowd ('So I said to Dali, "Salvador", I said — I always call him

Salvador ...'). He mingles happily with the outlandish guests at a party thrown by the eccentric artist Jim Smith (Dennis Price), including a yogi who is standing on his head (Hancock: 'I'd get you a drink but I thought you might pour it up your nose').

Paul — who actually has real talent — becomes discouraged and leaves for England; and distinguished art critic Charles Brouard (George Sanders) seeks out the now famous Hancock and mistakes Paul's paintings for Hancock's — dismissing Hancock's real efforts as rubbish by some other painter. Sucked into this deception, Hancock finds himself a celebrity, featured in newspapers and on the fronts of magazines in the exaggeratedly arty clothes he is now sporting. Brouard and Hancock are invited to stay on a millionaire's yacht at Monte Carlo ('Ah, Monty,' muses Hancock, 'one of the finest generals we ever had'). The millionaire buys all Paul's paintings (still being credited to Hancock) and commissions Hancock to sculpt his wife, with clear warnings about showing too much interest in her. As she is apparently a nymphomaniac Hancock is soon in a very worried state. At a fancy-dress party, to which he is going as a budgerigar (a reference to a TV sketch he performed some years earlier) he finally manages to convince her that he is not interested, whereupon she attempts to shoot him and accuses him of assaulting her. Escaping both from her and her husband's wrath at the completed statue (which is identical to the monstrosity he was working on at the beginning of the film) Hancock returns to London, where Brouard has arranged, without seeing them, an exhibition of Hancock's new paintings — genuine Hancocks this time. Knowing perfectly well what the result will be if his own infantile paintings are seen, Hancock persuades Paul to substitute *his* latest paintings. At the opening of the exhibition, Hancock is distraught to discover that Paul is now painting in Hancock's infantile style; but the paintings are acclaimed as masterpieces. Abandoning all pretences, Hancock introduces Paul as the real artist, and returns home to attempt his third statue, with a new model — Mrs Cravatte.

Despite the absence of an audience Hancock's timing and reactions are extremely effective, and the plot hangs together well (although the episode of the millionaire's wife seems rather unlikely, given the Hancock character). The film was very successful in Britain, although much less so in America, where the title was changed to *Call Me Genius*.

Hancock's next film, after several false starts with Galton and Simpson, was written by Hancock himself in collaboration with Philip Oakes. If Hancock was searching for something internationally acceptable, it is strange that he should have chosen to set his story in a small and run-down seaside town on the south coast, and to play a very British phenomenon — the proprietor of a Punch and Judy show.

The Punch and Judy Man was made in 1962 by 'MacConkey Productions' (Hancock's own company) and directed by Jeremy Summers; the script was written by Hancock and Philip Oakes. The story is set in the dismal seaside resort of Piltdown, where Wally Pinner (Hancock) is the Punch and Judy showman on the beach, and his wife Delia (played by Sylvia Syms) runs a china shop. Their relationship is somewhat strained because she hopes to get in with the important figures in the town — particularly the major (Ronald Fraser) and his wife — but feels that Wally's profession is holding her back.

In the first scene Wally is seen dressing to the accompaniment of the radio — complete with facial reactions to the programmes (*Housewives' Choice* and *Five To Ten*). At breakfast, the atmosphere is a little tense. Delia reads out some items in the paper, including a report on the doings of her favourite personality, Lady Jane Caterham (who had had to walk twenty yards when an airport bus broke down — Wally: 'What, you mean actually putting one foot in front of the other? Isn't that marvellous!').

Breakfast over, Wally and his assistant, Edward (Hugh Lloyd) set up on the beach, in the process inadvertently losing a customer for the roving photographer, Nevil (Mario Fabrizi), which leads to an argument. After exchanging greetings with the 'Sandman', Charles Ford (John Le Mesurier), who makes his living by creating sand sculptures of historical events and then lecturing on them, Wally embarks on his show. As it proceeds he exchanges comments with Edward, who is assisting. Asked whether he watches much television, he comments 'No, too much violence — very bad for the kids', meanwhile manipulating Mr Punch bashing Judy round the head with his stick.

The performance is rather spoilt by Nevil moving among the audience offering to photograph them, which causes Wally to lose his patience and end the performance early. This draws complaints from a small boy, Peter (Nicholas Webb) who — much to Wally's irritation — is present at every performance: 'You left the crocodile out!'

Meanwhile, the Mayor and Council are deliberating the special gala they are planning to celebrate Piltdown's 60th year. They decide to ask Lady Jane Caterham to switch on the illuminations; they also agree that the beach performers such as Wally Pinner and the Sandman are riff-raff who lower the whole tone of the place. Back at Delia's shop, the Mayor's wife — who is arranging the gala dinner — asks Delia if Wally will do a special performance of Punch and Judy for them. Delia is reluctant to commit Wally, but in the end agrees on the promise of being introduced to Lady Jane.

At lunchtime, Wally, Edward, the Sandman and Nevil repair to the saloon bar of the local pub. In the lounge bar they can hear the over-hearty laughter of some of the council members, and Wally embarks on a deliberate policy of annoying them. As he makes his way out to go home for lunch it is pouring with rain, and he spots the small boy, Peter, sheltering from the storm. Wally offers to lend him the bus fare home and to take him to the bus stop. He is slightly embarrassed when Peter takes his hand, but on the way they get side-tracked into an ice-cream parlour. Peter orders a Piltdown Glory ('two scoops of luscious vanilla, two scoops of tasty chocolate, a succulent slice of banana, juicy peach fingers in pure cane syrup, topped with super-smooth butter-fat cream. Oh — and a cherry!').

Finding that they do not serve either soup or tea, Wally — with some trepidation — orders the same concoction. Watching Peter carefully for the etiquette of eating it, he manages to get right to the bottom of the glass, including mimicking Peter's trick of tossing the cherry from the glass into his mouth.

The result of all this is to make him not only late for lunch, but unable to eat it when he does get home, much to Delia's annoyance. When he finds out that he is booked to appear at the gala dinner, Wally is even more annoyed, and flatly refuses; only after a good deal of heart-searching does he finally agree, not least because Delia is so anxious to go to the gala and meet Lady Jane.

Asking the Sandman to escort Delia, Wally and Edward take their equipment into the dressing-room of the town hall. He joins Delia and the Sandman as an extra guest for the dinner, first by stealing a chair from another guest (Gerald Harper) and then, when this ploy fails, persuading one of the waiters to find him a chair. Delia is upset because all evening she has been steered away whenever she tried to get near Lady Jane.

When the time comes for his show, Wally finds that he has the least sympathetic audience of his life. He is heckled by a drunk, and then, egged on by Lady Jane's bored (and drunk) escorts, members of the audience start throwing bread rolls first at Mr Punch and then at each other. In the ensuing chaos, Wally's booth is knocked over and blocks the exit Lady Jane is trying — with some disgust — to make. She and

Wally start shouting at each other, but when she reaches for a soda syphon as a weapon, Delia intervenes to protect him. Lady Jane slaps Delia — and Delia knocks Lady Jane clean out with a strong punch to the jaw.

The next morning the paper carries Nevil's photograph of the punch, and Delia is nursing both a black eye and her disappointment at the collapse of her social aspirations. However, she and Wally now have more sympathy for each other, and agree that they should move on to somewhere else.

The film is well conceived, and tells its story effectively. Hancock's performance is strangely muted — with the result that the film looks better on television than it does in the cinema — and the direction is rather flat. However, there are some excellent moments, in particular the opening scene of Wally dressing and then having a miserable breakfast, and the scene in the ice-cream parlour. Despite its flaws, the film shows the way Hancock was trying to go towards completely naturalistic comedy.

Hancock made only two more feature film appearances: although both films were international successes, he appeared only briefly in them and they made little use of his abilities. The first, Ken Annakin's 1965 comedy blockbuster *Those Magnificent Men in their Flying Machines*, adopted a thoroughly overblown approach to its subject that managed to diminish the efforts of most of its large star cast. Hancock appeared in a couple of very brief scenes, and seemed to be uninterested in the whole proceedings — certainly his performance is strangely detached. The film itself enjoyed considerable commercial success, but the real stars were the reconstructions of vintage flying machines.

Hancock's last film gave him a more satisfactory opportunity, although he still had only a fairly small role. Released in 1966 and directed by Bryan Forbes, *The Wrong Box* was based on a splendidly comic novel by Robert Louis Stevenson, and although the film tended to spoil matters by overdoing many of its jokes it still had many good comic moments. The involved plot revolved round the last two survivors of a Tontine — a strange form of lottery in which the total takings go to the last surviving subscriber. The venal nephews of one of the survivors — played by the already established comedy duo of Peter Cook and Dudley Moore — attempt to hush up the apparent death of their uncle because they believe (wrongly) that the other survivor is already dead and they want to claim the money. The complications mount as they try to dispose of the corpse they believe to be their uncle (but which is in fact that of a notorious murderer). The plot finally resolves itself into a chase involving the corpse, the money, three hearses and the main characters, all hotly pursued by an increasingly suspicious detective, played by Hancock.

Hancock made the most of his short role, as the detective becomes more and more exasperated when faced with the bedlam caused by the resolution of the chase, repeating his bewildered 'And who are *you*?' as each character is added to the final affray.

It was his last film appearance, and the hoped-for international recognition never came. Eric Sykes comments: 'It was a great pity that he never got *the* film that would put him on the international map. When you think of somebody like Dudley Moore — who is very funny and has tremendous charm and charisma — well so had Tony, and I think if Tony had had the same chances as Dudley Moore I think Tony would have been an international star. Of course Dudley has a lovely twinkle in his eye, whereas Tony was a bit austere. Dudley Moore, because he was small, tended to get a lot of sympathy — people wanted to cuddle him. I'm not sure that people wanted to cuddle Tony — Tony was always an arm's length away.'

Nowadays Hancock's hopes for international recognition can be set aside in the assessment of his work, and his two important films, *The Rebel* and *The Punch and Judy Man*, can be seen as among the finest of British comedy films.

Orders Are Orders *(1954). Though not the Hancock character well known from the later TV shows, Hancock's performance in this remarkably silly film is the best thing in it as he drills his military musicians.*

Orders Are Orders. *An historic first meeting. Sidney James (playing an unlikely American film magnate called Ed Waggermeyer) explains his cinematic visions to Hancock.*

Hancock's first major film role, in The Rebel *(1960),
starred him as a would-be artist who feels confined by his
humdrum office job. Here, in a scene not in the finished film,
he practises his craft copying a statue in a museum.*

The Rebel. *Released at the end of the day's work, Hancock rushes home to his rooms. The key to his bedroom is hidden in the post-horn in order to keep his landlady from seeing the illicit sculpture he is creating.*

TOP LEFT:
The Rebel. *Mrs Cravatte (Irene Handl) comes to investigate the strange banging sounds in Hancock's bedroom: 'I don't allow 'ammering in my rooms'. She is even less pleased with him when she sees the cause, and after an altercation tells him to get out.*

BOTTOM LEFT:
As with all films, the unit photographer on The Rebel *took a number of photos which were either purely for publicity or were of scenes cut from the final version of the film. Here, in a scene not in the film, Hancock poses with a picture quite unlike the ones his character paints.*

ABOVE:
The Rebel. *In another shot from a scene not in the film, Hancock trudges through the alleyways of Paris.*

The Rebel. *Hancock visits the eccentric artist Jim Smith (Dennis Price). Smith: 'I always think that an English name sounds so mysterious, don't you feel?' Hancock: 'Oh, yes, they do. I knew a Harry Trubshawe and a Bert Higgins once — dead mysterious, they were.' Smith has been sleeping on top of the bookcase. Smith: 'I prefer sleeping on soft wood — oak is so intense, don't you feel?' Hancock: 'Quite, quite — especially the knot-holes'.*

The Rebel. *At Jim Smith's party, Hancock explains to a crowd of beatniks why he had to leave London: 'You've no idea how frustrating it is to work with people of no imagination; they all looked alike, they all dressed alike, it was just a uniform!' As he leaves them, one comments to another: 'It must have been very soul-destroying to him; imagine, everybody looking alike. I couldn't live like that.'*

PREVIOUS PAGES — LEFT:
The Rebel. *Hancock describes his theories of art — all stolen word for word from his friend Paul — much to the admiration of the guests. Saying goodnight to Jim Smith — now sleeping in the fish-tank — Hancock goes home determined to emulate some of his host's strange habits, which include keeping a pet cow.*

PREVIOUS PAGES — RIGHT:
The Rebel. *Hancock waits between takes on the set of Jim Smith's party.*

RIGHT:
The Rebel. *After an uncomfortable night spent on top of the wardrobe, Hancock experiments with what is to him a new idea, an action painting. The cow — another idea borrowed from Jim Smith — watches suspiciously as Hancock sloshes paint about, dances on it and rides a bicycle over it.*

LEFT:

A publicity shot for The Rebel; *the painting is certainly not one of Hancock's.*

ABOVE:

The Rebel. *Clad in a budgerigar costume for a fancy-dress party aboard the millionaire's yacht, Hancock makes a panic-stricken getaway after the millionaire's wife has shot a pistol at him for rejecting her advances. Without changing he rushes to the airport and announces to a surprised clerk: 'I want to fly to London'. He is not amused to be told, 'It's a long way to London, m'sieu; you'd better wait for a plane'.*

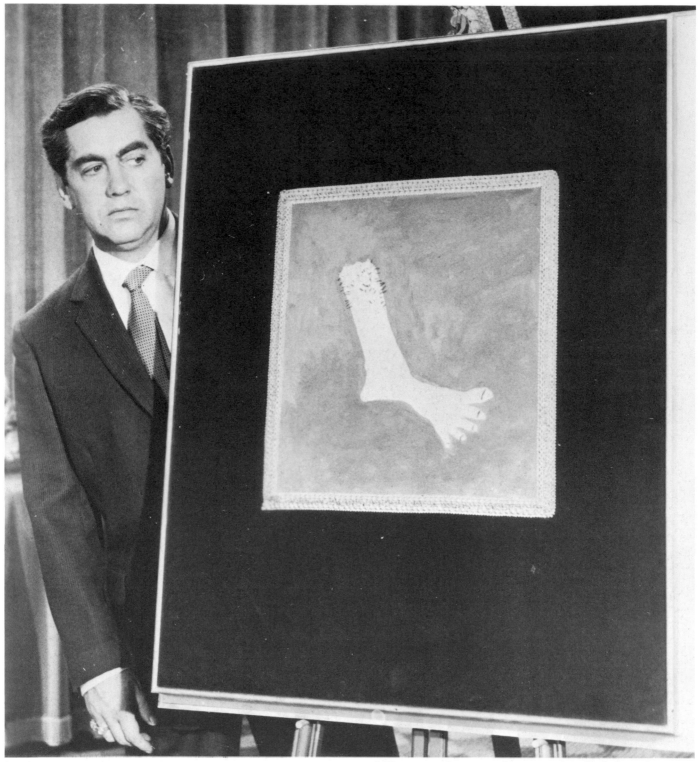

ABOVE:
The Rebel. *A London showing has been arranged of Hancock's latest pictures, only this time they really are Hancock's pictures, and not the ones which every one thought were his. Hancock looks worried, as well he might.*

TOP RIGHT:
2 March 1961. Hancock and Sid James clown for the press photographers at the London première of The Rebel. *Galton and Simpson, who wrote the screenplay, had wanted to include a brief appearance by James for comic effect, but Hancock refused, feeling that James was already well established in films and that he wanted to prove that he could make a success by himself.*

BOTTOM RIGHT:
Hancock and Trevor Howard meet at the Cannes film festival buffet.

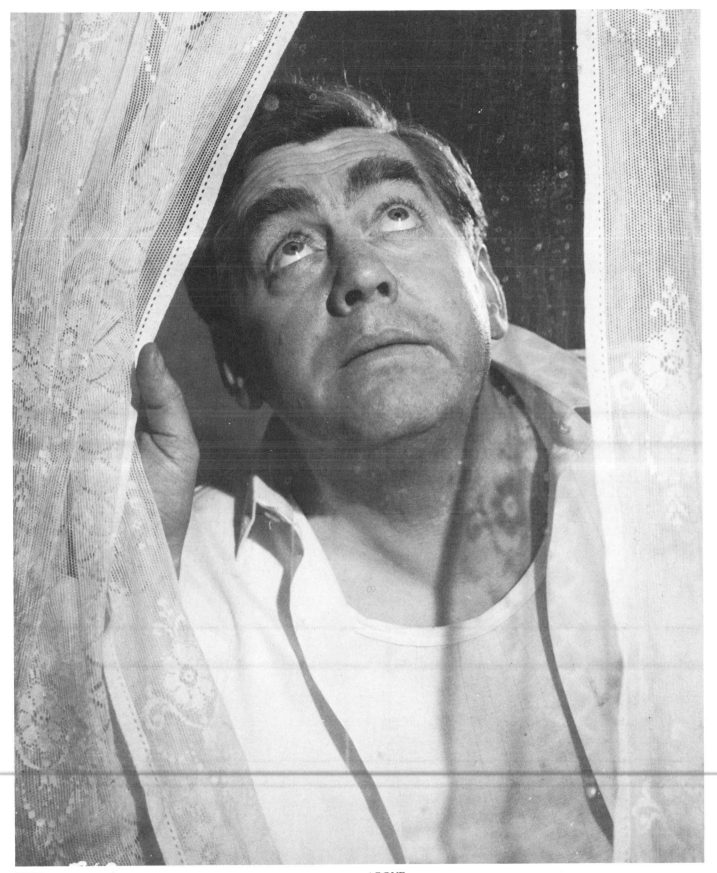

LEFT:
The Punch and Judy Man (1962). *Hancock poses with a co-star.*

ABOVE:
The Punch and Judy Man. *Wally Pinner looks out of his bedroom window at the start of an unpromising day.*

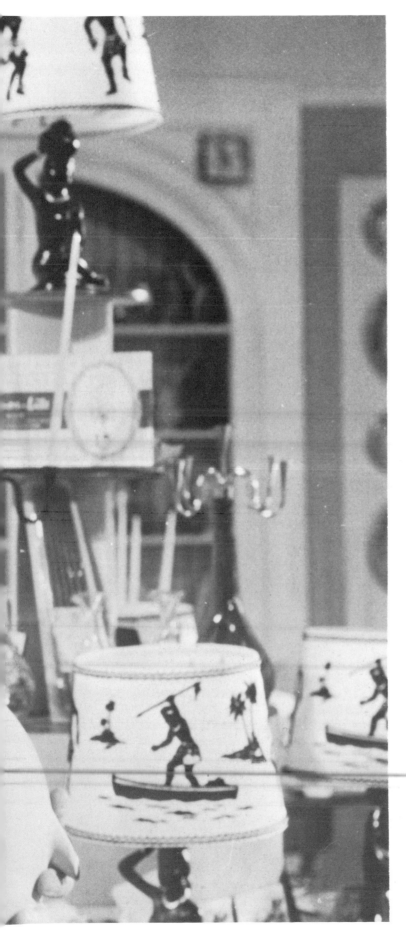

The Punch and Judy Man. *On his way out through Delia's shop after an uneasy atmosphere over breakfast, Wally gives vent to his feelings by planting flowers in an unconventional place.*

ABOVE:
The Punch and Judy Man. *The fortune teller (Hattie Jacques), Wally, and the Sandman (John Le Mesurier) in a scene not in the finished film; Hattie Jacques makes only a brief appearance.*

RIGHT:
The Punch and Judy Man. *Wally and the Sandman in the pub at lunchtime. From the adjacent bar comes the sound of hearty laughter. Wally: 'Hullo, the yaks are with us again'. The 'yaks' — mostly snobbish council members — resent his presence and the remarks he makes at them through hatches in the partition between the bars.*

The Punch and Judy Man. *Arriving for the gala dinner, by way of the artists' entrance round the back, Wally and Edward (Hugh Lloyd) find they have to carry their equipment upstairs.*

The Punch and Judy Man. *Wally and the Sandman at the gala dinner. Since the Sandman, who is escorting Delia, has come in on Wally's ticket, Wally should not be at the dinner-table, a problem he has solved by purloining another guest's chair (Gerald Harper). (The trick with the glasses is not in the finished film.) The ploy fails because, when they all stand for the Mayor's entrance, the guest steals his chair back and hangs on to it firmly.*

Those Magnificent Men in their Flying Machines.
Hancock as Harry Popperwell, who proposes to enter the London to Paris air race of 1910 by flying backwards ('less air resistance'). He is last seen heading in the direction of Scotland.

ABOVE:
The Wrong Box. *Hancock as the un-named detective in this version of Robert Louis Stevenson's comic romp, set towards the end of the 19th century. Here Hancock and his stalwart constables (Freddy Clark and George Hillsden) prepare to do their duty.*

TOP RIGHT:
The Wrong Box. *As the complications mount, Hancock arrests a suspicious character, the butler to one of the Tontine survivors (Wilfrid Lawson, turning in one of his usual magnificently inebriated performances).*

BOTTOM RIGHT:
The climax of The Wrong Box. *Hancock attempts to unravel the situation as the hearses, the body, the money and the rest of the cast converge on the graveyard.*

Any actor will confirm that most film work consists of waiting around for 95 per cent of the time. Here the technical staff on The Wrong Box *line up a shot; Hancock waits.*

ABOVE:

Hancock and Dudley Moore chat between takes on The Wrong Box. *In a way an ironic photograph, for Moore — then known only for his British TV appearances with Peter Cook — was later to go to Hollywood and achieve exactly the kind of international comic stardom which Hancock hoped for. Moore's self-deprecating charm was more easily assimilable by the Americans than Hancock's complex character could ever have been, but no one could doubt that Hancock at his best was by far the greater comic.*

RIGHT:

Looking more like a Mafia employee than a 19th-century detective, Hancock waits to be called for a shot in The Wrong Box.

EPILOGUE

Photograph by Harry Secombe

It is unfortunate that to the popular press, and to some more serious writers, Hancock's personal difficulties have always been more interesting than his work and his extraordinary comic ability. Hopefully, with the new availability of the BBC television material after so many years there will be more likelihood that it will be the performances which remain in the public memory. There can be no doubt that Hancock was one of the very greatest comic actors ever; his innate ability to phrase a line, to time a pause, to express his thought with that mobile face and to create a memorable and likeable character whose very faults made him endearing must surely place him in a class with the other great performers — Chaplin, Sid Field, Keaton, W.C. Fields, and Laurel and Hardy. All of those except Sid Field had the Hollywood machine behind them; and Chaplin had a steely ego and an exact knowledge of what he was doing which made him less susceptible to the pressures of his work. As physical comedians, the Hollywood performers had a better chance for the international appeal which Hancock could never attain — and perhaps never would have, even had his difficulties not prevented him making a more successful attempt. But Hancock, unsuited to Keaton's acrobatics and deliberately eschewing Chaplin's sentiment, made a direct appeal to his viewers which has placed him high in the affections of the British public in a way which few other performers have ever managed.

Even in the much changed world of modern television comedy Hancock's work stands head and shoulders above anything else on television. Eric Sykes: 'Comedy these days is more frenetic — it isn't the gentle, time-to-pause comedy that we had in those days. Now it's all bang-bang, and everybody's shouting and rushing about . . . there's nobody of any depth — they're what I call flavour of the month. Well Tony wasn't flavour of the month, he was there to stay and he has done — he was on a par with the greats as far as I was concerned.'

Hancock was unique — his performances were instinctive, his ability to create a comic character unparalleled, and the affection with which he is held untarnished by the many years since his best work. The comedy he created is timeless and will remain as a peak of achievement as long as the recordings which are his memorial still exist.